Larry Winget has already helped countless people to get ahead in life. Here's what a few of them have to say about him and his program:

"With Larry's help I got myself out of massive debt, quit my underpaying job, and got my life in order. Larry's harsh manner is a reality check and a swift kick in the rear to get your life in order. While Larry's tough love and advice is hard to swallow initially, he is a lifesaver!!!"

—JEWEL PENA

"Larry has a no BS approach. Some people might find him rough around the edges, even offensive, but when you think about everything he has personally overcome, you'll see that he knows what he's talking about! We are living proof that his philosophy works!"

—GREG AND SUE COSCINO

"He's not only been where we were, he's done what it takes to fix it. He has this type of passion to help those who are serious about changing their lives. Yes, Larry is a very blunt, in-your-face hard-ass. But if you listen to him, what he says makes sense and his ideas really work. Before Larry, we didn't think we were ever going to get ourselves out of our financial mess. But after listening to Larry we could see the light at the end of the tunnel."

—NICK AND BECCA

YOU'RE
BROKE
BECAUSE
YOU WANT TO BE

YOU'RE BROKE BECAUSE YOU WANT TO BE

How to STOP GETTING BY and START GETTING AHEAD

LARRY WINGET

GOTHAM
BOOKS

GOTHAM BOOKS
Published by Penguin Group (USA) Inc.
375 Hudson Street, New York, New York 10014, U.S.A.
Penguin Group (Canada), 90 Eglinton Avenue East, Suite 700, Toronto, Ontario
M4P 2Y3, Canada (a division of Pearson Penguin Canada Inc.); Penguin Books Ltd,
80 Strand, London WC2R 0RL, England; Penguin Ireland, 25 St Stephen's Green,
Dublin 2, Ireland (a division of Penguin Books Ltd); Penguin Group (Australia),
250 Camberwell Road, Camberwell, Victoria 3124, Australia (a division of Pearson
Australia Group Pty Ltd); Penguin Books India Pvt Ltd, 11 Community Centre,
Panchsheel Park, New Delhi – 110 017, India; Penguin Group (NZ), 67 Apollo
Drive, Rosedale, North Shore 0632, New Zealand (a division of Pearson New
Zealand Ltd); Penguin Books (South Africa) (Pty) Ltd, 24 Sturdee Avenue, Rose-
bank, Johannesburg 2196, South Africa

Penguin Books Ltd, Registered Offices: 80 Strand, London WC2R 0RL, England

Published by Gotham Books, a member of Penguin Group (USA) Inc.

First printing, January 2008
10 9 8 7 6 5 4 3 2 1

Gotham Books and the skyscraper logo are trademarks of Penguin Group
(USA) Inc.

LIBRARY OF CONGRESS CATALOGING-IN-PUBLICATION DATA
Winget, Larry.
    You're broke because you want to be: how to stop getting by and start
getting ahead / Larry Winget.
        p.   cm.
    ISBN 978-1-592-40334-9 (hardcover)   1. Finance, Personal.   I. Title.
    HG179.W5473   2008
    332.024—dc22   2007033838

Printed in the United States of America
Set in Janson Text
Designed by Sabrina Bowers

While the author has made every effort to provide accurate telephone numbers
and Internet addresses at the time of publication, neither the publisher nor the
author assumes any responsibility for errors, or for changes that occur after publication. Further, the publisher does not have any control over and does not as-
sume any responsibility for author or third-party Web sites or their content.

This book is for my wife, Rose Mary.

She stuck with me through thick and thin. (Even when the thin was so thin it became transparent!) She watched me lose, she watched me win. She believed in me when no one else did and when I forgot to. She is my rock.

A party gives laughter,

And wine gives happiness;

But money gives everything.

—*Ecclesiastes 10:19*

CONTENTS

YOU'RE
BROKE
BECAUSE
YOU WANT TO BE

THE DIFFERENCE BETWEEN POOR AND BROKE

BEFORE WE BEGIN, LET'S MAKE SURE WE UNDERSTAND ONE ANOTHER.

Don't start in on me because of the title. Please don't say, "But what about the poor people, Larry? They don't *want* to be broke."

Great point. You're right. I'm not talking about being poor.

Poor is a condition I find very sad. Sad, yet inevitable. Jesus said, "The poor will be with you always." And they will. There are people who live in societies and countries where there are no opportunities for advancement and it takes all their effort just to survive. They are not going to have enough to eat well or live well or take care of themselves.

So let's get this straight from the outset so you can get off your high horse and understand what I am really saying. I didn't write this book for the poor people of the world. I know it is going to take a lot more than a book to help truly poor people. To think otherwise would be insulting.

I am talking about broke. Broke is not a condition like being poor. Broke is a situation you find yourself in because you are either underearning or overspending. I can't fix poor, though I would love to. I'm good, but I'm not *that* good. I can fix broke. That's what this book is about. Read it and find out how to fix your situation so you don't have to be broke any longer. You can get ahead and live the way you want to. I'll show you how, step by step.

I wrote this book for the average person who has a job, makes a living, and still can't seem to get ahead. If you're someone who dreams of being rich but can't quite seem to turn your dreams into reality; if you're ready to turn your life around and finally have financial freedom; if you are buried in debt and can't stop living paycheck to paycheck; if you spend more than you make and can't figure out how to stop doing it, this book is for you!

Got it?

NOW, BACK TO THE TITLE.

You read it right. You are broke because you want to be.

"How can you say that? You don't even know me! There is no way you can sit there saying that I want to be broke when you have no idea who I am!"

Here is how I know:

> If you didn't want to be broke,
> you wouldn't be broke.

It's as simple as that. What you say you want means almost nothing. When every action you make contradicts your words, your words don't mean a damn thing!

This may be a new idea for you, or not. It doesn't matter! Aligning our intentions with our actions is something we can all learn to do better. It is the key to unlock your potential, get out of debt, and get ahead in life. It is something you can learn, but in exchange you have to give something up.

VICTIMHOOD: A PRIVILEGE YOU CAN NO LONGER AFFORD.

Stop being a victim! No one else is to blame for your situation. Broke didn't sneak up on you in the night. A stack of unpaid bills didn't show up while you weren't looking. You didn't suddenly get behind. You chose to spend your money the way you did.

Your life is a reflection of the choices you have made. If you want a better life, then make better choices. When you do, you'll find that taking credit for your successes feels a lot better than blaming others for your failures.

If you are desperate to improve your financial situation, then this book is a great place to start.

WHY SHOULD I LISTEN TO YOU, LARRY?

I have a television show on A&E called *Big Spender*. The show is about people who are in financial crisis due to their spending habits. I ambush them in the middle of a spending spree and confront them with the mess they have created. I go through their finances and give them a plan to turn their money and their lives around before everything crumbles around them. The show is not about investing or the stock market or any sophisticated financial solution. It is about rescuing people from the hole they have dug before it turns into a grave.

There are shows that teach you how to invest and what to invest in. That's not what I do. I force people to confront their situation and then give them a concrete plan for improving their situation immediately. That's what I know how to do, and that's what I'm good at. In fact, all I really know about money is how to make it, how to enjoy it, and how to make sure there is always plenty of it. Isn't that what you want to know? Isn't that what you are most lacking? I bet I'm right.

As important as that, however, is this: I've been

broke. Really broke. I was so broke I couldn't even pay attention.

Later I'll give you the details of what happened to me and what I did about it, but here is the overview of why you should listen to me:

I grew up dirt poor.
I decided to get rich.
I got rich.
I went bankrupt.
I learned from it.
I became a millionaire.

There is my credibility: failure—success—failure—success. Real world. No silver spoon, no golden parachute, no pie in the sky BS and no get-rich-quick schemes. Nothing but work: work on my thinking, work on myself, and then just plain old work!

I know what I'm talking about. I've done it. And I can teach you how to do it too.

A WORD OF WARNING:

I am not a blow-smoke-up-your-skirt, you-can-do-anything-with-a-positive-attitude kind of guy. I am a nose-to-the-grindstone, no-excuses-will-be-accepted kind of guy. I'm harsh. I'm abrasive. Your feelings will probably get hurt as you read what I have to say. I'm not the guy you go to so he can put his arm around you and say, "That's okay, it will be all right." It's not okay and chances are it won't be all right. I'm the guy you go to when you are circling the drain. I'm the guy you go to when everything else has failed and you are desperate. I know what it's like to be desperate because I've been there. It's terrifying. And the last thing you want is a hug and to be told to have a positive attitude. I believe you want real answers and are willing to forgo the niceties to get them.

WHAT THIS BOOK ISN'T.

This is not an investment book.

I don't know enough about investing to write a book. I have no clue how the stock market works and I don't care. I hire real experts who have even more money than I do to advise me on my investments. When you have money, that's what you should do too.

This is not one of those cutesy parable books.

Like the ones that preach at you about being rich and then suggest you live a pauper's lifestyle. Why work hard to become a millionaire and then live like a pauper? Where's the incentive in that?

I am also not going to tell you "I want you to be rich" like some authors do. The reality is, it doesn't matter what they want or what I want. Until *you* want to be rich, nothing will change for you.

This book isn't one of those new-agey, money-is-a-spiritual-concept books.

I won't teach you to develop your prosperity consciousness or get beyond your poverty consciousness. And I am not going to tell you to touch your chest or head and repeat affirmations like some authors do. While I believe completely in those concepts, this just isn't that kind of book.

Affirmations are fine, but affirmations alone don't change your life. You can say, "I am rich, I am rich, I am rich" until your face turns the color of money, but until you stop doing stupid stuff with your money and start doing smart stuff with your money, you will still be broke. Affirmation without implementation is self-delusion.

Most people can't identify with those approaches because they are just too far in the hole for those books to have any practical application. When you are trying to figure out how to keep your ten-year-old beater from being repossessed, it's hard to focus on the chauffeur-driven limousine you would like to own.

And as for that big "Secret" that has become the most popular book and DVD on the planet, I have an issue. *The Secret*'s basic philosophy is: What you think about and talk about comes about. That's fine, but it's only part of the story and will leave you short on results. A secret that gives you only half the instruction manual is worthless. You want the *real* secret? Here it is: What you think about, talk about, and get off your ass and do something about comes about.

Telling someone that they can think themselves rich makes as much sense as saying you can think yourself thin and healthy. At some point, you have to put down the ice cream, get your fat butt off the sofa, and do some exercise. Think thin and eat a package of Twinkies and see how much weight you lose. Think rich and blow your rent money on shoes and eating out and see how that works for you. If you act in contradiction to what you think, you will end up worse off than you were to begin with.

The *Real* Secret!
What you think about, talk about, and get off
your ass and do something about comes about.

Do you need this book?

Do you spend more than you earn?

Do you worry about how you are going to pay
your bills?

Are you barely getting by?

Do you live paycheck to paycheck?

Are your credit cards maxed out?

Do you have a shopping problem?

Do you have little or no savings?

Is Social Security your only retirement plan?

Do you have more debt than you can afford to
make payments on?

Are you terrified of an emergency that would
leave you financially devastated?

If you missed a paycheck, would you be screwed?

Are you clueless about how to fix your situation?

If you answered yes to even one of those questions,
you need this book!

THIS IS WORK!

Going from getting by to getting ahead is tough—really
tough. I went from broke and bankrupt to millionaire
and every step was a hard one for me. It still is. But it
can be done.

The principles I am going to teach you in this book are the principles I use to this day and still find challenging. Rich is never easy unless you are one of Trump's kids or your last name is Hilton. Most of us aren't born that way. We have to work for it. This book is about work. I won't sugarcoat it.

Books don't make you rich. Sooner or later, like it or not, it always comes down to work. Sadly, most people won't put in the time or the effort to get what they want. I don't make many guarantees in life or in my books. But I will make this one: If you stick with me during these pages, fill out the forms, and dare to do what I ask, then you will be better off financially. Maybe you won't be a millionaire, maybe not even a thousandaire, but you will be better off financially than you are right now. I promise.

ONE LAST THING:

The work I'm talking about begins with this book. This book is a *work*book. You will find lots of blanks for you to fill in. Fill them in. You have to read this book actively in order for it to do you any real good. You can't become successful passively. I don't believe you should read a book passively either.

Your first assignment is to get a highlighter to highlight passages you want to remember. Second, get a pencil or pen to fill in the blanks. Third, actually fill in the blanks.

If you skip the work, you only cheat yourself and chances are you have been doing that way too long already.

Okay, let's get started. And as I say on my television show, *Big Spender*: It's about to get ugly!

PART ONE

WHY YOU'RE BROKE

1) Think and grow Rich —
   Napoleon Hill

2) Manifest your destiny —
   Dr. Wayne W. Dyer

3) Creating Affluence —
   Deepak Chopra

4) You were born Rich —
   Bob Proctor

5) why youre dumb, sick and broke —
   (also) smart, healthy + rich — by
   Randy Gage

6) Rich dad poor dad — Robert T. Kiyosaki
7) Start late finish rich — David Bach
8) Never Eat Alone — Keith Ferrazzi
9) The Millionaire Zone — Jennifer Openshaw
10) Go put your strengths to work —
    Marcus Buckingham
11) Its called work for a reason./ your success is
    your own damn fault / shut up stop whining. Larry Winget

CHAPTER ONE

MONEY MATTERS

So you want to stop being broke and start getting ahead?

Bullshit.

(Okay, I warned you. I don't mince words. That was a pretty hard slap in the face. Do yourself a favor and get over it. You have a problem and need help or you wouldn't be reading the book to begin with. Work with me and let's fix your problem together. Listen to what I have to say. I know what I'm talking about. After all, I've been where you are and now I'm rich.)

You want to be broke because you are. If you wanted to stop being broke, you would have done something about it already. You haven't, therefore you don't want to.

DON'T TELL ME WHAT YOU WANT.

I already know what you want. You want your life to be exactly like it is.

> You want to be a person who just barely scrapes by, because you do.
>
> You want to be a person who pays bills late, because you do.
>
> You want to be a person who mooches off of others, because you do.
>
> You want to be a person who buys things you can't afford, because you do.
>
> You want to have a car you can barely pay for because it makes you feel better about yourself, because you do.
>
> You want to wear the hottest new fashions instead of paying your rent, because you do.
>
> You want to spend instead of save, because you do.
>
> You want to eat out instead of saving for your kid's college education, because you do.

People do what they do because they want to do it. Period. Do this little exercise for me: Quickly turn your head from side to side. Did you see anyone on either side of you holding a gun to your head forcing you to do the stuff you are doing? If no one is forcing you to do it, then you must be doing it because you want to. It's as simple as that.

Go ahead and get mad at me now for saying what I just did. In fact, I *want* you to get mad. While you are getting mad, think about this: Are you mad at me and what I've just said or are you mad at yourself because you know I'm right?

"I DON'T REALLY WANT TO BE *RICH*, I JUST WANT TO BE COMFORTABLE."

Comfortable means that you don't feel bad but you don't feel all that great, either. Most people are comfortable. That's the problem. Comfortable people don't feel bad enough to change but don't feel good enough to really be able to enjoy their lives. Either way, their future is doomed.

People never make changes in their lives when they are comfortable. You have to get uncomfortable in order to make a positive change in your life. This book is supposed to make you uncomfortable.

> You will never change
> until you first become uncomfortable.

"MONEY ISN'T ALL THAT IMPORTANT TO ME, LARRY."

Yeah, right. People say that to justify the fact that they don't have money. In fact, the *only* people I have ever heard say that were broke. Money is important.

People who don't have money can't help anyone. Hospitals are built with money. Charities are funded with money. Homeless people are fed with money. So get some money so you can do your part. You owe it to yourself and you owe it to the world.

Imagine this: You are sitting on your sofa watching the television coverage of a disaster. Something like Hurricane Katrina has just happened and you want to help. You would love to write a check for a thousand dollars, or ten thousand dollars, or maybe even just ten dollars, but you can't—you're broke. When you are rich, you have the freedom to do that kind of stuff. Which does more good—wanting to help or being able to help?

"But, Larry, I send good thoughts and I pray for those people."

Good for you. Send your good thoughts and say your prayers, because they are important. Then write a check. The world needs your good thoughts, your prayers, *and* your money!

> "Keep on succeeding, for only successful
> people can help others."
> —Dr. Robert Schuller

MONEY DEFINES YOU.

Some of you will have a real problem with that statement. The fact that I said those three words will upset some people so much they will call me shallow, greedy, and lots of other uncomplimentary things. However, you can argue with that statement all you want and I will still be right.

When you think of Diddy or P. Diddy or Puff Daddy or Sean Combs or whatever his name is this year, do you think of him as an African American, a male, an entertainer, a movie star, a fashion mogul? Or do you think of him as rich? I'm betting rich. Is he a good person? Is he benevolent? Is he a total jerk? Beats me—I don't know him. I do know that he's rich.

Donald Trump. What immediately defines him? His hair? His real estate? His television show *The Apprentice*? Sorry, those things don't come to mind first when you think of him. It's his money. He is rich. Love him or hate him, those thoughts come after you think of how rich he is. Money defines Donald Trump to each of us.

Money determines the neighborhood you grow up in. It determines the clothes you wear to school. Money usually decides who your friends will be and how others will treat you. Money decides whether you will go to college or not. Money usually even picks the college. Money determines the house you live in, the car you drive, and the clothes you wear. It determines whether you get a good doctor or an amazing doctor. It determines whether you hire an ambulance chaser or the best defense attorney money can buy. It determines every restaurant you go to, every store you shop in, and every entertainment activity you attend. Money even determines the size of your gravestone and the quality of the casket you will be buried in.

Fair? Probably not. But life simply isn't always fair. It is what it is. This is reality. I don't make the rules, I just try to figure them out, play by them, and win in spite of them.

Money has defined my life. My lack of money while growing up is what made me who I am today. It motivated me to become the best at whatever I was doing and to work harder than most others so I could make plenty of money and not be poor. Going bankrupt made me even more determined to get rich again. Now the presence of money in my life defines me to the point that I have the credibility to do a television show about money and write books about how to be successful. Am I more than that as a person? Of course I am. I'm a good husband to my wife, a good father to my boys, and a good son to my momma. I'm a mediocre golfer, a great decorator, and a pretty good cook. I design my own cowboy boots and I can paint a room better and faster than anyone I know. I am a lot of things other than rich. But money still defines my life.

Money defines your life, too.

My point with all of this? Never say money doesn't matter.

MONEY *ALWAYS* MATTERS.

While money always matters, sometimes people expect too much from money. There are many things that money won't do for you.

Money won't bring you happiness.

Happy people are happy whether they have money or not. Happiness is a choice. Let's not give money much credit when it comes to being happy or not being happy. There are rich people who are happy and rich people who are miserable. But at least rich people are miserable in a better part of town!

Money won't buy you friends.

The friend that money can buy isn't much of a friend. When the money goes, so will the friend. Money can buy you companionship, though. Don't believe me? Walk through any casino in Las Vegas and look at the rich old geezers with the eye candy on their arms. Those little hotties aren't there because they find potbellies, bald spots, and yellow teeth charming and fascinating. So if it is shallow companionship you are looking for, then money can help. True friendship is never bought and paid for.

Money won't solve your problems.

More zeroes does not mean fewer problems. Bad things happen to rich people just like other people. People who have money worry, too. Sometimes they even worry about money.

Money doesn't mean you will pay your bills on time.

People who pay their bills on time do so because that is the kind of people they are. If you don't pay your bills on time when you are broke, then you won't pay your bills on time when you are rich. The newspaper is full of stories about rich movie stars who don't bother with their taxes or who are being sued because they didn't pay their house-keeper or their bills. These people can afford to do the right thing; they just aren't the kind of people who do the right thing.

Money won't make you more charitable.

People who are charitable are that way regardless of income. I find it interesting that the people who are most charitable, in terms of percentage of income given to charity, are people of moderate income. Ask a bartender or waiter who the best tippers are. It's not always the rich guy who orders the bottle of Dom Pérignon; it's usually the regular guy who has a regular job.

Money won't give you a better marriage.

While money problems are the number one cause of marital problems, having lots of money won't guarantee you a better marriage. People with a bad marriage usually have a bad marriage for lots of reasons. I have talked with many couples who say the only problem in their relationship is money. Usually, it doesn't take long to find out that money is the least of their problems.

One couple I worked with on my TV show had been dating and engaged for ten years but had never had a discussion about money. They were planning their wedding and had no money saved. They were living on payday loans, had accounts in collections, were months behind on their rent, and each year were spending tens of thousands of dollars more than they earned. They had even had a car repossessed. According to them, their only problem was they didn't make enough money. But it looked to me like they had commitment problems: After all, they had been together ten years and hadn't gotten married. They had communication problems: They had never had a conversation about their money. They lacked discipline, had problems taking responsibility, and had integrity issues because they didn't bother paying their bills or their rent on time. This couple was a mess on every front, yet it was easier to blame money than for them to take a good hard look at themselves.

If this is your situation, I'm sorry. Get some counseling and go to work on both your finances and your relationship.

Money won't make you successful.

Success is about much more than money. Success is all-inclusive. Success is having good relationships, fulfilling employment, and being as healthy as you can be. Yet while money is not success, success certainly requires money.

Money won't make you a better person.

If you are an asshole when you are broke, you will be an asshole when you are rich. You will just be an asshole with money.

There are good people and there are bad people. That is reality.

Good people pay their bills. They are charitable. They do the right thing regardless of circumstances, whether anyone is watching or not. They work. They have integrity. They are honest. They honor their commitments and obligations. They take responsibility for their words and their actions. They take care of their families.

Bad people don't do those things.

People are the way they are because that is the way they choose to be. Money doesn't change the kind of person you are. You are who you are because of the choices you make, not because of how much money you have.

Money magnifies everything.

Having money is like holding a magnifying glass up to every aspect of your life. If you are a good person who does good things when you have only a little, then you will be a good person who does even more good things when you have a lot. If you are a rude, discourteous, arrogant asshole, that is who you are with or without money; money just makes you more noticeable.

In fact, magnification is what gives money a bad name. We watch moronic rich people on TV and we blame their money for making them stupid. If Paris, Britney, and Lindsay weren't rich, they would be still be crashing their cars and acting stupid at Wal-Mart instead of on Rodeo Drive. You just wouldn't know about it. When you see rich people doing ignorant things, don't blame the money. Money doesn't make you stupid; it just gets your picture taken more often.

> "Most of the things money is the root of ain't evil."
>
> —Malcolm Forbes

WHAT WILL MONEY DO?

Money will allow you to spend money when you want to, give money when you want to, and have financial security.

That's about it.

"Wait! That's it? You had a whole long list of what money won't do and you only give me one sentence about what money will do?"

Yep, that's it. All money will do for you is give you a little freedom and a little peace of mind. Trust me, that is enough to make it all worthwhile!

"But you don't understand!"

Now you are going to offer up the excuses, aren't you? Well, don't. Just don't.

I've never found an excuse I could get behind or buy into. Know why? I can always find someone worse off than you, someone with problems bigger than yours, and they still figured out a way to be rich and successful. If one can do it, so can another.

SOME OF THE COMMON EXCUSES FOR BEING BROKE:

"I grew up poor."

Having money is not the result of your environment. There are more people who have earned their millions than have inherited their millions. Lots of millionaires grew up with nothing. My grandfather was a carney. Seriously. He worked at a traveling carnival with a bear, a monkey, and a pony ride. Later he lived in a storeroom in the back of a furniture store. My parents never had much. Yet I still got rich.

It's not how you start out that matters, it's how you end up.

"God will provide."

Saying that is like going on vacation and leaving your doors unlocked. It's not smart. Do that and even God would think you were being stupid. God already provided for you by giving you the ability to earn a living. Don't blame God for your situation or expect God to show up with the grocery money. Instead, get off your lazy butt and go to work!

And while we are talking about God, let's cover another popular excuse:

"It's God's will."

What kind of God do you worship who wants you to be broke? If you think God wants you to be broke, you need a new God. After reading just about every book representing most of the world's religions that I could lay my hands on, I haven't found anything that would make me believe that God wants you to be broke. Don't ever get sold on the belief that it is God's will for you to have anything less than all there is.

"I'm a single parent. I work hard. It takes all I've got just to get home, fix dinner for the kids, take a bath, and get some sleep."

This is a tough one. I know there are lots of people in this situation and I'm sorry. But it can be overcome if you want to overcome it. There are too many stories of single mothers and fathers who work two and sometimes three jobs, put themselves through night school, and finally move from getting by to getting ahead and then rich. You can do it too, if it means enough to you. So I am not going to let you off the hook. I am going to understand, sympathize, and then ask you: "So with all of that going on, how many hours of television did you watch last week? Couldn't you have been reading a book? Isn't there something you could have done to increase your worth to your employer or to yourself? Couldn't you have been learning some marketable skill?" Ouch! We all think we work so hard, there is just no time for anything else. Yet a study I found about media consumption says that the average American will spend:

    65 days per year in front of the television
    41 days listening to the radio
    7 days on the Internet
    7 days reading the newspaper
    7 days listening to music

That's plenty of time to read a book, take a class, or do some work on yourself. Something that would make you worth more in the marketplace.

> "If you feed your mind as often as you feed your stomach, then you'll never have to worry about feeding your stomach or a roof over your head or clothes on your back."
>
> —Albert Einstein

I readily admit that there are lots of hardworking people out there who never get rich. I get it. Two hardworking people raised me, so it's hard for me to get too far down on people who work hard and are still pretty much broke. But I will. It takes more than hard work. It *starts* with hard work but it still takes more. It takes the willingness to do whatever it takes to get ahead.

My son Patrick is a fashion designer. He works as many hours and about as hard as anybody I've ever seen. Early in his career, when he was trying to figure out how to make a living doing what he was doing, he learned to live on practically nothing. He did all of his shopping at the dollar store. He worked eighteen to twenty hours a day. He learned to eat on twelve dollars a week. Luckily, he could make his own clothes! He would go to the fashion trade shows in Las Vegas and while his buddies in the business were staying in suites at Mandalay Bay and

Caesar's Palace, he was at the Howard Johnson's paying $39 a night, sharing a room with his business partner, and eating rice cakes, beef jerky, candy bars, and five-for-a-dollar sodas they had bought at the dollar store. Now he makes good money and I predict he will be a millionaire in the next few years. But he paid his dues. He sucked it up and did what it took to survive regardless of how inconvenient it was. Along the way, he learned to speak Mandarin Chinese, Spanish, and a bit of Japanese so he could communicate with his suppliers and manufacturers. Now he says he wouldn't trade those days for anything because of the lessons he learned. The lessons he learned could fill a book, and knowing him, someday they will. Really, who can eat on twelve bucks a week in Los Angeles?

While I admire what my son has been able to accomplish, I really told that story about him to get to the story of Joel, who worked with Patrick. Joel moved to the United States from Guatemala to make a better life for his family. He had a job sewing garments in a large garment factory in Los Angeles. He rode the bus an hour to get to his job, which started at 7:00 A.M. and ended at 5:00 P.M. He then rode the bus back home to eat with his family and at 7:00 P.M. boarded another bus to a movie theater, where he took tickets until 10:00 P.M. He then got on another bus to travel to Patrick's place, where he sat at a sewing machine until 1:00 A.M. sewing samples for Patrick. At that point, Patrick would drive him home.

He did this six days a week, and many times, seven days a week. According to Patrick, he never complained and was always happy, cheerful, and thankful just to be able to have three jobs so he could help his family go from getting by to getting ahead.

There are millions of stories like Joel's. Stories like this make me very intolerant of people who complain about their lot in life and how hard they work on their one job. You do what you have to do because it is the right thing to do for your family and yourself. You do it because you want more. You do it because you can. Success and prosperity are rarely, if ever, easy. Success takes lots of hard work.

"I deserve to spend my money the way I want!"

I believe you deserve to be financially secure, have some savings, and be able to enjoy the money you have. You deserve peace of mind. With those two sentences, I have just proven that I think more of you than you do of yourself.

"I'm too far behind to ever get ahead."

No, you aren't. It may be ugly for you and things may be truly bleak, but you can always get ahead. I am not going to insult you by telling you it will be easy. At times, digging out of your mountain of debt to get ahead will be overwhelming. But know this: You can do it if you want to do it. You may not be able to make your life perfect, but you can certainly make it better than it is. The biggest mistake you can make is to believe that your situation is hopeless. It's not hopeless because you aren't helpless. Accept responsibility for where you are and then go about fixing it. Give yourself a little credit; you're reading this book, aren't you?

"I don't know how to get ahead. No one ever taught me."

A woman once told me her father said to her that as long as you dress really nice, wear a Rolex watch, and drive a Mercedes, then nothing else matters. I told her that her father was an idiot. To teach your kid something so totally stupid is criminal in my opinion. I felt sorry for this woman—for about a minute. She was almost thirty years old. At some point you know what is right and wrong regardless of what your parents did or said to you.

I helped another couple who told me that neither of their parents was ever good with money, therefore they weren't. Okay, that excuse flies. But only to about the end of the block and then it crashes and burns with the rest of the excuses. I understand that we are all products of our environments to some extent. That works until you are about thirteen years old; then you should be able to look around and figure some things out for yourself. When you are thirty-five years old and still blaming your parents, you need a reality check. Grow the hell up.

"I'm not good at math."

I had a guy tell me the reason he couldn't get ahead and pay his bills was because he wasn't good at math. Lousy excuse. Especially since this guy was only working nine hours a week! Math wasn't his problem. Work was his problem. I'm not talking about advanced algebra. Just write down how much you make and then below it write down how much you spend. If the number on top is smaller than the number on the bottom, there is a problem.

"It's the credit card companies' fault."

Believe it or not, that is a popular excuse I hear often. One woman told me that the reason she had so much debt and was on the verge of bankruptcy was because the credit card companies kept sending her preapproved applications. She told me if they didn't send the applications, she wouldn't feel compelled to take the cards and charge things. Consequently, she had fifty-seven credit cards and owed nearly $100,000.

Credit card companies are not to blame for your situation. You are. When the applications come in the mail, don't open them. Don't fill them out. Shred them.

"Stuff happens."

Yes it does. But if you are blaming your lack of money on the uncontrollable circumstances of life, then you are lying to yourself. I know things happen. When I was flat broke, my dog's knee blew out and her knee replacement cost me $1,200 I didn't have. Was it the dog's fault that I was broke? Was the world plotting to get back at me because of my lack of money? Was it the veterinarian's fault that it cost so much to replace the dog's knee? No, it was *my* fault I was broke. Your indebtedness is due to your lack of control over your spending. When an emergency comes along, you should have the savings on hand to take care of it.

"But, but, but . . ."

Get your buts out of the way and admit that the reason you don't have any savings to take care of emergencies is because you spent it on other things. You chose not to sock away a few bucks like you should have. It's not the fault of the emergency. It's your own damn fault.

"Things cost too much."

I know how much things cost. I know the price of a gallon of gas and a gallon of milk. I am not one of those guys who doesn't do his own shopping and doesn't have a clue. I go to the mall and the grocery store and pump my own gasoline just like you do. Yet I can still promise you that things do not cost too much. Things just cost what they cost. Besides, you have no control over what things cost. Deal with it. Don't whine about it. Your problem is not what things cost; your problem is that you don't earn enough money to pay for the things you want. You can't control what things cost; you can control your money.

"I don't have a high-paying job."

I hate it when people say stupid things like "Of course he's rich, he's a doctor." Or "She owns her own company; no wonder she drives a Mercedes." "He's a ballplayer; of course he drives a Lamborghini." (Okay, that last one works.) Your job won't make you rich (unless you are a ballplayer). There are broke doctors and lawyers and dentists and lots of broke company presidents. And there are rich truck drivers and janitors and factory workers. I've helped a bankruptcy attorney married to a mortgage broker who were on the verge of bankruptcy. I've worked with mortgage underwriters who were so broke and their credit was so bad, they couldn't buy a house. I even helped a CPA who had never kept a personal check record. See the irony in those situations? Jobs and money have little to do with each other. Don't blame your job for the fact that you don't have any money. It's not your job's fault. It's your fault.

"But I don't have any skills."

Whose fault is that? Get some skills. Read a book. Go to night school. Take a correspondence course. There are lots of ways to get skills. Some are even free. Besides, you already have the skills to do better. You could get an extra job with the skills you already have. If financial security is important to you, you should be willing to do whatever it takes regardless of the inconvenience.

YOU ALREADY KNOW WHAT IT TAKES TO DO BETTER.

There are only three reasons people don't do well in life. They are stupid, lazy, or don't give a damn. Which fits you?

First, you aren't stupid. You may do stupid things, but you aren't stupid. Every person with a heartbeat knows at least one thing they could do to be more, do more, and have more. Let me prove it to you. I am going to ask you to look at several areas of your life and write down one thing you know you could do to make it better. I will help you by giving you an example. I want you to add one to what I give you. Be specific, because you know yourself better than anyone does.

THE ONE THING I KNOW THAT WOULD IMPROVE MY RESULTS:

AT WORK.

Larry's one thing: I will work every minute they pay me to work.

My one thing:

WITH MY FAMILY.

Larry's one thing: I will stop parking myself in front of the television and instead spend time with my family.

My one thing:

WITH MY SIGNIFICANT OTHER.

Larry's one thing: I will tell her something I appreciate about her every day.

My one thing:

TO BE A BETTER PARENT.

Larry's one thing: I will spend at least twenty minutes a day talking to my kids in real conversation about things they are interested in.

My one thing:

WITH MY HEALTH.

Larry's one thing: I will eat a little less and exercise a little more every day.

My one thing:

TO BECOME SMARTER.

Larry's one thing: I will read a nonfiction book about how to be more successful. (Good news, this one counts!)

My one thing:

WITH MY FINANCES.

Larry's one thing: I will stop spending money on things I don't absolutely need.

My one thing:

_____

_____

See? You know at least one thing you could do in each area I have listed. You even know something you could be doing to improve your financial situation. The problem never is that you don't know what to do. The problem is that you don't *do* it. In other words, you are lazy! And you don't care. I don't get this at all! I don't understand how anyone can know what it takes to do better in life and not care enough about themselves or their family to do it.

WHAT'S YOUR EXCUSE?

Did I miss yours in my list of excuses? I might have. It would have taken a hundred pages to cover all of the excuses people use for not having enough. In addition to those I've listed already you could probably add:

the government

my boss

my husband

the economy

my employees

my wife

the system

my customers

my ex-husband

my geographic location

my coworkers

my ex-wife

my environment

my ethnic origin

my children

the politicians

my church

my parents

my education

my religion

my in-laws

the weather

my company

my family

So what's yours? What are the excuses you use for your financial problems? Write them down.

MY LIST OF EXCUSES FOR BEING BROKE:

Without even looking at what you have just written, I can tell you that there is a problem with your list. *You* aren't on it. That's right. The list of reasons for not doing well in your life is actually a very short list. It should contain only your name. Why don't you just go back and add it?

> "People do not want to take responsibility for the scarcity in their lives. It is much easier to blame circumstances, others, events, or even God for the things they have failed to acquire or achieve."
> —Dr. Wayne W. Dyer

In the next chapter, find out how to stop making excuses and start solving the problems that are really holding you back.

CHAPTER TWO

YOUR REAL PROBLEM

THE BIG SHOCKER:

You don't have a money problem.

"I don't have any money; to me, that seems like a problem."

The fact that you don't have any money is a result of all your other problems. You have thinking problems. Attitude problems. Self-esteem problems. You are lazy. You lack discipline. You lack integrity. You don't take responsibility. You lack goals. Your priorities are out of whack.

Your biggest problem is not in your wallet or your bank account. Your biggest problem is between your ears. You will fix your money problems when you fix your other problems. That's what we are going to address right now.

SPEND YOUR WAY TO RICH.

"This doesn't even make sense, Larry. You can't spend your way to rich. Spending is what made me broke!"

No it isn't. Spending didn't make you broke. Spending on the *wrong things* made you broke. When you learn to spend on the right things, then you will be rich.

> "Almost any man knows how to earn money, but not one in a million knows how to spend it."
> —Henry David Thoreau

I dealt with a couple on my television show, *Big Spender*, where the wife had $600,000 worth of clothes. That's not a misprint. She had $600,000 worth of shoes, purses, and clothes. She had over four hundred pairs of designer shoes and three closets full of clothes separated by designer label! The couple didn't own a house. They spent much more money than they earned. Their credit rating was pathetic. They were living in her mother's house rent-free, in order to save for a house, while her mother lived with her grandmother. But they had spent all the money they were supposed to be saving on designer shoes and clothes and owned not one thing that mattered long term. They could have paid cash for three $200,000 houses! Instead, they had nothing. Spending didn't kill their financial future, but spending on the wrong things did.

I never quit spending even when I was flat broke and bankrupt. I did quit spending on things with no future value, though. Eating out? We stopped. New clothes? We stopped. Cable television? It went away. My wife and I made a deal that we would spend money on only one thing: getting smarter. I bought books. I would skip a meal and skip watching television, but I wouldn't skip an investment in my brain. I knew that investing in success would pay off. And it did. After twenty years and nearly four thousand books, I am beginning to figure some things out! Education is not an expense; it is an investment.

THE $30,000 MILLIONAIRE.

When I was a little boy I saved up my pennies to order Sea-Monkeys from an ad in the back of a comic book. They looked *so* cool—happy little creatures smiling and swimming around in their little castles. I (and a million other little boys) found out, much to our dismay, that the precious little sea monkeys we were hoping for were nothing more than nasty little brine shrimp kicking around in dirty water. I got ripped off but I learned a valuable lesson. Things are not always as advertised.

And that is the story of the $30,000 millionaire. You know the kind: the guy who earns thirty grand a year and yet tries to look and live like a millionaire. He has one cool outfit, a pair of $300 sunglasses, and parks his AMC Gremlin down the street from the highest-priced, classiest bar in town, then walks in like he owns the place and maxes out his third MasterCard trying to impress others. As they say in Texas, "All hat, no cattle."

The $30,000 millionaire is a person who puts all his effort into looking rich rather than actually being rich. If he put as much effort into being rich as he did in looking rich, he just might find himself rich.

FOLLOW THE MONEY.

Just like in a crime drama, politics, or a good murder plot, the key is to "follow the money." Money is a dead giveaway of what is important in anyone's life. What do your bank statement and credit card statements say about you?

I was working with one family when I asked the father if he loved his son. He said of course he did. I told him he didn't. I told him that he loved his cigarettes more than he loved his son because he spent more on his cigarettes than he did making sure his son had a secure future. I then took his cigarettes from him, threw them on the floor, and stomped them flat with my cowboy boot. He was pissed! I loved it. And I was right. It doesn't matter what you say is important to you, your actions always tell the truth. When you follow the money, you know what someone really loves.

If you spend hundreds or even thousands of dollars at the mall to make sure you look fashionable and cute, then looking good is important to you. That's fine. Look as cute and fashionable as you can afford to look. But if you do that instead of making your car payment or paying your utilities or putting away money for your future or your kid's education, then you have messed-up priorities.

I asked a guy who was in deep financial trouble what was important to him. He said, "Having fun, my family, and my wife." Gee, I wonder why he was in trouble? He put having fun ahead of everything else in his life. And that's exactly where his money went. He owed for his student loans, owed family members, and owed lots of other creditors, yet he spent money on gadgets and plasma-screen televisions and partying with his buddies and never even bothered to open his big basket full of bills.

I dealt with another couple who had spent $70,000 on their wedding. Then they did a thirty-year refinance on their house to come up with the money to pay for it and their other credit card bills. I told them that on their thirtieth anniversary they could break out the champagne and toast the fact that they had finally paid for their wedding.

Am I against expensive, fancy weddings? No, but for that couple the expense was out of scale with their income. One day of happiness and some good pictures and then thirty years to pay it off doesn't compute.

You have to get your priorities straight before you ever are going to get your money straight. You need a written-down list of exactly what is most important to you. You do have that, don't you?

"I just live. I have the stuff I have the money to pay for, or the stuff they will allow me to charge. My life is just the way it is. I don't have a list."

There is your problem! No list. We are going to fix that now. Make a list of what is important to you. Write down everything that really matters to you.

WHAT IS IMPORTANT TO YOU?

_____

_____

_____

_____

_____

Okay, that's what you say is important to you. Get your bank statement and your credit card statements and write down where you spend your money. Then you will know what is really important to you.

_____

_____

_____

_____

_____

See any difference between the two lists? Are you willing to do what it takes to get your actions into alignment with your priorities?

IT'S EASIER THAN YOU THINK.

This is how I did it: I decided to get rich.

It happened when I was thirteen years old. I walked into civics class in the eighth grade wearing my only pair of blue jeans. They weren't Levi's like all the cool kids had. They were Roebucks. Remember Roebucks? Most people have never even heard of Roebucks. They were the Sears store brand jeans back in the '60s. My dad worked for Sears, Roebuck and he got an employee discount, so I had to wear the cheapest jeans that we could buy at a discount. My parents couldn't afford more than that one pair of blue jeans for me.

The jeans had a tear on one of the pockets. The significance of that tear was that it made it obvious that I only had one pair of jeans. One day one of the kids in my class said to me, "Winget, you wear the same pair of jeans every day. Can't you afford more than one pair of jeans?" He said it in front of a lot of people and, most importantly, a lot of girls I would have done anything to impress. I tried to laugh it off and say that I had lots of jeans and somehow I tore them all in the same spot. But I was still busted. I knew it and they knew it. My parents were great people and doing what they could, but the bottom line was that I was a poor kid with only one pair of blue jeans to wear to school every day. I hated it. At that moment, in Muskogee, Oklahoma, at Alice Robertson Junior High School in eighth-grade civics class, Larry Winget decided he was going to be rich. While I had no idea how I would ever be rich, I knew I would do anything not to be poor. I couldn't bear the humiliation of being poor and having people know it. That decision shaped my life. I got rich at that moment. It took me more than thirty years to make it happen.

After my decision to get rich, I began taking action. I got a picture in my mind what rich looked like, felt like, and smelled like. I started writing things down. I made lists with details of how I wanted to live and what I wanted to have. I affirmed wealth. The first thing every morning that came out of my mouth was, "I am happy. I am healthy. I am rich." Still is. I learned to celebrate every prosperous thing that happened to me. I stopped focusing on what I didn't have and started focusing on what I did have. While I didn't have much, I had the willingness to do whatever it took to get ahead. And what it takes that most people aren't willing to give is work. Hard work. Work on yourself, work on your life, and working while you are at work.

In college, I did several things to make money. I raised houseplants from cuttings and sold them out of my driveway on weekends. I tied macramé pot hangers and sold them as well. My fingers were covered with blisters from tying so many. I was a telephone operator from 10:00 P.M. until 7:00 A.M. I then drove an hour to get to college, where I attended classes from 8:00 A.M. until 3:00 P.M. I came home and went to sleep for a couple of hours, got up and did my homework, and then tied macramé for a couple of hours. Am I bragging? Sort of. I'm proud of it. I worked. I was usually tired, burned out, and worn out. But I was willing to do whatever it took to get more out of life. As I look back I realize that I was never too good to do anything I needed to do to change my circumstances. There are people who have done much more than I have done and overcome odds much worse than mine to become rich. Stop thinking you are different or that your story keeps you from getting rich. Your story, regardless of how bad it might be, is not unique.

I'll bet you are disappointed now, aren't you? You wanted more than some guy telling you to decide to be rich and then work your ass off to get there. You wanted some complicated strategy for wealth. I don't have one. I simply wanted to be rich, I decided to be rich, and I was willing to work as hard and as much as I needed to make it happen.

WHY IS MORE IMPORTANT THAN HOW!

> "He who has a why to live for can bear with almost any how."
>
> —Friedrich Nietzsche

In the second half of this book, you will learn how to realize your goals. I'll give you the steps it takes to make them real. But knowing "how" makes little difference without knowing "why"! *Why* is the motivator, the incentive, and the thing that keeps you sticking with it even when you don't feel like it. *How* is the work. *Why* is the reason to do the work.

Why did I get rich? I owed it to myself. I owed it to my family. I wanted it. I knew I could do it. I didn't want the humiliation of having less than I could have. I wanted to know that I could achieve anything I decided to achieve. I wanted to live better than anyone in my family had ever lived. I wanted to travel, stay in nice hotels, and eat at great restaurants. I wanted to shop at expensive places and drive amazing cars. I wanted to be able to send my kids to any college they wanted to attend. I wanted my wife to have anything she wanted. I wanted a house that others would look at and say, "Wow!" I wanted to be able to help others by giving to charities that touched my heart. Those are just a few of my "whys." What are yours?

WHY DO YOU WANT TO BE RICH?

PART TWO

HOW TO START GETTING AHEAD (MAYBE EVEN RICH!)

CHAPTER THREE

KNOW WHERE YOU ARE

Of all the people I have worked with on their money and money problems, there has yet to be one—I mean *one*—who knew how much money he earned and how much money he owed. You can't get ahead until you know what you have to work with.

It's time to figure out exactly how much you owe.

This is where you make a list of every dime you owe and who you owe it to. I mean all of it. That hundred bucks you borrowed from your brother-in-law goes on the list. This is also the place where you write down your other monthly expenses. Anything you spend money on such as groceries, gasoline, eating out, going to the movies, pet care, and more all go on the list. Don't just write down what you think you are spending; go from actual expenses. Check your bank records, receipts, and credit card statements. This is not the place to fudge the results; this is the place to tell yourself the cold, hard, ugly truth about your money.

MONTHLY

Mortgage or rent _____
Car loan #1 _____
Car loan #2 _____
Personal loans _____
Other loans _____

CHARGE ACCOUNTS:

MasterCard _____
Visa _____
Discover _____
American Express _____
Other credit cards: _____
   #1 _____
   #2 _____
   #3 _____
   #4 _____
   #5 _____

MONTHLY EXPENSES:

Insurance _____
Electricity _____
Gas _____
Water and trash _____
Telephone _____
Cell phone _____
Cable television _____

Internet _____
Other utilities _____
Gasoline _____
Groceries _____
Eating-out _____
Gifts _____
Dry cleaning _____
Health club _____
Hobbies _____
Vacation/travel _____
Clothes _____
Entertainment _____
Personal care _____
Pet care _____
Charity _____
Medical _____
Savings/
investments _____
Church/charity _____
Alimony/child
support _____

Any other debts
or expenses: _____

**TOTAL DEBTS
AND EXPENSES** _____

Now it's time for you to figure out exactly how much you earn.

THE MONEY YOU HAVE ON HAND:

Cash on hand   _____
Checking account   _____
Savings account   _____
Tax refunds due you   _____
Money owed you   _____
Other   _____

TOTAL   _____

This is what you have to work with other than your regular monthly income. Sadly, the total above is probably going to be pretty low because most people just don't have much money on hand. So let's move on to the number you really have to work with.

HOW MUCH MONEY I TAKE HOME (AFTER TAXES) EVERY MONTH:

Monthly income: _____

Now let's do a little basic math:

Monthly income: _____

Minus monthly expenses: _____

Your financial picture: _____

Here is a hint: The number on top should be bigger than the second number, leaving you with an excess of money each month. If you are currently making less per month than you spend each month, then you are in deep doo-doo. It either means you aren't paying your bills or you are living on credit cards.

Shocked? I have done this exercise with many people and I've never met anyone who wasn't shocked by how much money they were spending. I have shown people they were spending twice what they earned and they didn't have a clue. I have sat with people who thought they were spending only about $1,000 a month more than they earned, only to prove to them, based on their true expenses, that they were spending nearly $7,000 a month more than they earned.

> **If your outgo exceeds your income,
> then your upkeep becomes your downfall.**

So, how much short are you?

Write it down _____

If you aren't short, then how much more do you make than you spend?

Write it down _____

HOW DOES THIS MAKE YOU FEEL?

Capturing the emotion of how you feel right now is important. Take a minute and write down how you feel after finally discovering your true financial picture.

_____

_____

_____

_____

_____

_____

_____

_____

_____

_____

_____

_____

TAKE RESPONSIBILITY FOR YOUR SITUATION. EXPERIENCE REMORSE!

I am talking about good ol' "Holy crap, I'm an idiot!!" remorse. I want you have the kind of remorse where you wallow in the mud, feel like a moron because you are, cry, apologize, and think there is no bigger dumb-ass on the planet. I want you to go to the mirror and look at yourself with tears running down your face and bemoan the fact that you and only you are to blame for all your problems. I want you to hurt and hurt bad! I want wailing and gnashing of teeth of biblical proportion.

Why? Because it's honest. If you are spending more than you make, are in debt because you can't control your spending, and earn less than you could, then you deserve to feel the pain of your choices. I believe pain is a much better motivator than pleasure. Don't believe me? Think of Jack Bauer on the television series *24*. I love that show and chances are you have seen it. If you haven't seen it, just know that Jack Bauer is a Bad-ass with a capital *B*. When the boogeyman goes to bed at night, he looks under his bed to see if Jack Bauer is hiding there. If Jack Bauer sat you down in a chair and said to you, "Tell me where the nuclear bomb is and I'll send you on an all-expenses-paid vacation to Tahiti," or if he tied you in a chair, held a pair of wire cutters to your hand, and said, "Tell me where the nuclear bomb is or I'm going to cut off your fingers one by one and watch you bleed to death," which would get your fastest and most honest response? See what I mean? Pain is always a better motivator than pleasure.

Plus, remorse is the first step toward accountability. When you feel bad for doing something, you are taking responsibility for the action.

On my A&E reality series, *Big Spender*, I confront people with their financial problems. Some of them cry. I like it when people cry. In fact, I love it when people cry. Not because I'm a bully who enjoys watching tears run down someone's face but because it shows me that they have finally attached some emotion to their mistakes. They are feeling the pain of their decisions. When that happens, they have a shot at changing.

In one episode, I dealt with a guy who was a moocher. He mooched off his parents and his fiancée. He drove a car that was in his fiancée's name. He carried a credit card that was also in her name because his credit was too bad to get his own. He carried another credit card that was in his mother's name to buy all of his gasoline. He lived with his fiancée in a house that was in her name and he didn't contribute one dime toward the house or any of the household expenses. He ate out nearly every meal because he didn't like to cook, eat leftovers, or eat frozen food. He was a grown man acting like a spoiled baby. I confronted him with his mistakes and gave him the verbal spanking he deserved. I was all over this guy. It got ugly! I made him sob and boo-hoo until he finally admitted his mistakes. It was painful for him. (Sometimes, Jack Bauer looks under his bed to see if *I'm* there!) At the end of the day of shooting, he wanted to quit. He didn't see any way he could continue, because he didn't want to go on national television and appear to be the bad guy or look stupid. The problem? He *was* the bad guy and had been very stupid. I told him while there was no way to change the past, no one would judge him poorly if he turned it all around in the future. I was giving him a chance to look like a hero instead of a bad guy. He had already done the hardest thing of all: He had taken responsibility for making the mess and he felt bad about it. The rest, while tough, is never as tough as that first, all-important step.

In my own life, when my back was against the wall and there was literally no place to turn, I went to see a bankruptcy attorney. The attorney talked to me about options, but explained after reviewing my case that I didn't really have any. Because of the business I owned 15 percent of, and my willingness to sign the loans, which included my personal guarantee on each of the loans, I was toast. So off to bankruptcy court I went. If you've never been, trust me, it's not a place you want to go. Some of my creditors even showed up. I had to talk to them and answer their questions. I had to look them in the eye and admit to them and everyone in the courtroom that I was a deadbeat and couldn't pay them the money I had agreed to pay. One of them even yelled at me and wanted to know what kind of a person I was to get myself in that condition. I didn't have an answer. My head was hanging so low that I couldn't even look up past my feet. I was disgraced. I had let my family down, ruined our credit, and embarrassed myself. My bankruptcy filing came out in the newspaper. Everyone I knew was aware of what I had done. I had been branded a loser and a failure. I could not imagine feeling worse. I was left with two choices: wallow in it or get past it. I decided to get past it. I sucked it up and went to work doing anything I could to make a buck.

That humiliation motivated me. The pain of going through that experience made me know that I was never going to feel like that again. I made a commitment to get rich *again*.

Feel the pain. Know what you cost yourself and your family. Know how your irresponsibility is going to affect your life for a good long while—maybe forever.

Then, after you feel appropriately remorseful, wipe away the tears, suck it up, and get mad about it. Anger can be a very healthy emotion when used to motivate yourself into positive action. Get angry and fight back. Yep, I said fight. You are in a battle. You need to steel your confidence with anger. Be angry that you messed up. Be angry that you didn't keep your word to your creditors. Get mad at yourself for all your mistakes. Get sad, get mad, and then get on with it.

The progression for moving forward:

Remorse ⟶ Anger ⟶ Determination!

COME CLEAN.

If you are part of a couple who is in financial trouble, this is the time to come clean about all of your expenses. No hiding things. You need to know where you both are, so get it all out in the open and deal with it.

I worked with one couple that was in real trouble. She was a shopping maniac. Her husband knew about her debts, or so he thought. Behind his back, she borrowed $30,000 from her mother to consolidate some of her credit card expenses. He was clueless about this transaction. I exposed her deceit on national TV and he was, to say the least, pissed off. But not as pissed off as I would have been. I can be tolerant of almost anything other than purposeful deception and lying.

You need to work together on your problem or your problem simply won't get fixed. One person in the couple can't do it alone. If only one person in the partnership tries to fix it alone, then he or she will begin to resent the other person and the relationship will suffer because of it.

When I crashed and burned financially, my wife and I circled the wagons and worked together to fight our way back. We opened up the lines of communication like never before. We plotted and schemed and presented a united front to our creditors and to the world. It made our marriage stronger. In fact, it is one of the things that has sustained us through the years when we have faced any number of problems.

KNOW WHERE YOU WANT TO BE.

I have been in the self-help business for nearly twenty years. Over that time I have talked with thousands of people one-on-one about their lives. I used to get letters and now I get e-mails—hundreds of them each month—from people who want to ask me questions about how to better their lives. Most just want to explain how bad their lives are. They don't really want to get better. I actually write most of these people back personally. My favorite question to ask them is, "Did you have a plan to lead a life that is so messed up? Did you write down that you wanted to be broke? That you wanted to be stuck in a dead-end job? That you wanted to be trapped in a crappy marriage? That your kids would be a mess?" I know their answer will be, "No, of course not!" I then ask, what was their plan? I know the answer to that one, too. They didn't have a plan.

None of the people I've helped on my television show has had a written-down plan. Not even a 3×5 card with one sentence on it. Not a Post-it note. Nothing.

And they wonder why their lives are such disasters. Isn't it obvious? They don't have a plan for their life to be anything *other* than a disaster. Do you?

Nobody ever wrote down a plan to be broke.
Broke happens when you don't have a plan.

How much money you would like to earn?

_____

How much money would you like to have in savings?

_____

How much money would you like to give to charity?

_____

How much money would you like to have in an education
account, an emergency fund, etc.

_____

How would you like to dress?

_____

Where would you like to travel?

_____

At which restaurants would you like to eat?

_____

What kind of car would you like to drive?

_____

What would you like to own?

_____

What kind of house would you like to live in?

_____

What part of town would you like to live in?

_____

You get it by now. So what do you want? How would you like to live? Write it down:

_____

_____

_____

_____

_____

_____

_____

_____

_____

_____

_____

_____

Just like the title of the book says: You're broke because you want to be. You can also be rich because you want to be—but only if you are willing to take action.

CREATE AN ACTION PLAN TO GET
WHAT YOU WANT.

It's not enough to just know what you want. If you only focus on wanting things, you will end up with more want. You have to have an action plan: things you can do every day to move yourself closer to your goal. It is important for you to know what you want in the future, but now you need to put your energy into the present. Always ask yourself what you could be doing *right now* to make sure you have the future you want to have.

MY ACTION PLAN:

To be fair, you probably didn't write much down in that section because you simply don't know where to begin. That's okay: I'm about to help you with that. Read on.

CHAPTER FOUR

HOW TO GET OUT OF DEBT

Time for the real how-to stuff now. It's time to take some real action on your life and your financial future.

If you want to turn your life around financially, it's really very simple. It comes down to two things: You have to either reduce expenses or increase income. Which should you do? <u>Both</u>. To really get ahead, you have to spend less money and earn more money—it's not enough to do just one.

Here are the steps you should take right now to help you do just that:

STOP SPENDING.

THE HOLE PRINCIPLE.
When you find yourself in a hole—stop digging.

It doesn't make sense to go any deeper in debt. So don't. Plug the holes. Stop the hemorrhaging. Spend money only on the necessities. What are the necessities?

> **Shelter.** Your rent or your house payment. This includes utilities.
>
> **Food.** That means eating conservatively . . . at home!
>
> **Bills.** Your obligations. Money you have *already* spent that must be paid back.

Those are the necessities: a roof over your head, food in your tummy, getting out of debt. And remember, no new debt!

KEEP A JOURNAL.

Part of knowing where you are is to keep a journal of your expenses. Get a little blank book or even a spiral notebook. Put the date at the top and draw a couple of vertical lines. Write down what you spend your money on and exactly how much everything costs. Keep track of every penny that flows from your hands on a daily basis. Track the categories of your daily expenses: gas, food, clothes, shelter, utilities, insurance, entertainment, and stupidity. Yes, stupidity is a category, too. We all have things we spend our money on that are just flat-out stupid. When you start tracking your stupid stuff and see how it adds up at the end of the month, you will be less likely to spend your money in stupid ways next month.

JOURNAL PAGE EXAMPLE

DATE	ITEM	AMOUNT SPENT	CATEGORY
7/22/07	M.H. Properties	$933.33	rent
7/22/07	FastPass monthly payment	$246.38	commute
7/23.07	movie	$10.50	entertainment
7/23/07	popcorn at movies	$4.50	stupid
7/23.07	dinner	$22.75	entertainment
7/24/07	groceries	$17.13	food
7/24/07	gas	$20.00	commute

CUT UP THE CREDIT CARDS.

You knew this was coming. This is old, worn-out news. So stop right now; go get your purse or your wallet and a pair of scissors and start cutting. Keep one card for emergencies. And a trip to the mall is *not* an emergency. (I once told a young woman that she had to cut up her credit cards but could keep one for emergencies. She picked her Neiman Marcus card. Holy crap! All I could do was shake my head and tell her to cut it up.) You get to keep one of the following: a Visa, MasterCard, American Express, or Discover. Something you can use *anyplace* when you have a real emergency—I'm talking broken bones or blood, something that requires medical attention.

I am not anti–credit card. I have several. But I pay them off when the bills come in. That's the rule. If you can't pay it off when the bill comes in, or at least the following month, then don't charge it. Old balances cost you way too much in interest.

Notice I didn't say, "Cancel the credit card." I said cut it up. If you have a credit problem, then cutting up the card means you won't have the card to carry around and you won't be able to use it to increase your debt. No card, no way to use it. Very simple.

THE THREE MOST IMPORTANT NUMBERS IN YOUR LIFE.

Surprisingly, those numbers are not your IQ (assuming yours hits the triple digits). Those three numbers are your credit rating.

> There are two things you will never be without:
> One is your reputation and the other is
> your credit rating.
> You can ruin both in an instant, and you may
> never be able to fix either.

Your credit score determines whether you can get a loan and how much you will pay for the loan. It's important. Over a lifetime it can either save you hundreds of thousands of dollars or cost you hundreds of thousands of dollars. It can even have an impact on whether you get a job or not. Your former employer won't legally be able to tell me whether you are a responsible person, but your credit score will. Protect your credit score at all costs. It is going to be with you forever.

A bad credit score never really goes away. You can take the steps to fix it and the bad ratings will drop off eventually, but if creditors dig deep enough, those little dings will still always be there like a dark cloud hovering over you.

Note: It is impossible to give you a specific number of what constitutes a good credit rating. Scores range from 350 (rare) to over 800 (equally rare). I'll just say that your number needs to be in the mid-600s for you to qualify for a decent interest rate on a home or car loan. But a swing of even 20 points in either direction can make a huge difference in the amount of money you end up paying over the life of your loan. Your overall goal should be for a rating in the 700s.

To find out more about your credit score, contact any of the three major credit reporting bureaus:

Equifax: www.equifax.com
Experian: www.experian.com
TransUnion: www.tuc.com

CALL YOUR CREDITORS.

The most common mistake people make with their creditors is to stop talking to them. They hide from them. They duck creditors' phone calls and ignore their letters. Stop doing that. Take the initiative and open up the lines of communication.

That's right, get on the phone and talk to them.

Credit is judged on two things: willingness and ability to pay. If you haven't been paying your bills, then you have already demonstrated to your creditors that you don't have the willingness to pay. Let them know you are now willing to pay them. Talk to them about your ability to pay them and negotiate the best deal you can for repayment of your debt.

Don't pay someone else to call your creditors. The "credit doctors" will happily call your creditors to negotiate on your behalf, but they don't do this for free. There is a charge involved and sometimes it is hefty. Want to know why they can charge so much to do it? Because they know how much you don't want to do it. Don't pay someone else to clean up a mess that you made.

SET PRIDE ASIDE.

When a creditor calls asking for money that is due, don't be defensive. This is a huge mistake most people make when it comes to dealing with their creditors.

Thirty years ago I worked in the business office for Southwestern Bell, calling people about their telephone bills. I got yelled at, cussed out, and called names just for asking people to pay their bills.

I learned some things from that job about paying your bills. If a late payer would just tell the truth and admit that he messed up, take responsibility, say he was sorry, and send me any amount of money no matter how small, I would leave his telephone turned on. Lie to me and the next time he reached for that phone, he wouldn't hear that sweet little dial tone in his ear; he would hear only the deafening sound of silence.

Don't forget it's *your* fault you are behind on your bills, not the fault of your creditors. Your creditors are only doing their job when they try to collect from you. Their job sucks. They have been lied to, cussed at, and heard every excuse in the book. Be nice to them. Shoot them straight and send them some money. Never make a promise you don't intend to keep. Work *with* them, not against them, and you might find them pretty easy to get along with. You need your creditors on your side, so don't alienate them.

Try this: Pay everybody something, even if it is just a little bit. The ones with the highest interest rates get the most. The one with the smallest interest rate gets the minimum payment. But everyone gets something.

WARNING!! SLOW TRAFFIC AHEAD!

Getting out of debt and becoming financially secure is a slow process. Just like getting into debt was a slow process. It takes some time. Don't get depressed and disillusioned because it is taking so much time to pay things off. Chances are you have very high interest rates and most of your payments are going to interest. That means it will take a long time before you ever even hit the principal. Don't give up. You nickel-and-dimed your way into debt and you are going to have to nickel-and-dime your way out.

Get a calendar.

Get one with squares big enough to write in. Write down the day each bill is due. When you make the payment, write PAID in bright red across it. I can't begin to tell you the relief you will have when you see a calendar full of big red PAIDs written all over it. It will make you sleep better, that's for sure.

Pay what you agreed to pay, when you agreed to pay it. It's an issue of integrity. Paying your bills late makes you a liar. The credit card company agreed to extend you the credit and you agreed to make your payment on the designated day. You even signed a contract saying that you would abide by the terms of the agreement and pay your bill on a certain date each month. If you aren't doing it, then you have lied. It's as simple as that. You aren't holding up your end of the bargain.

CALENDAR PAGE EXAMPLE

MON	TUE	WED	THU	FRI	SAT	SUN
1 Rent due **PAID**	2	3	4	5 Electric Bill due *PAID*	6	7
8	9	10	11	12	13	14
15 Visa Bill *PAID*	16	17	18	19	20 Cable bill due	21
22	23	24	25	26	27	28
29	30	31 Insurance due	1	2	3	4

Pay your bills as they come in.

Don't save your bills and pay them all at once. First, that makes it a chore. And we all do our best to avoid a chore. Second, a big stack of bills can be overwhelming. Instead, when a bill comes in, pay it. It only takes a minute and will give you a feeling of accomplishment that you are paying your way out of debt on a regular, almost daily basis.

Make little payments on your payments.

This is a trick I learned years ago when I owed a lot of people a lot of money. When a bill comes in, let's say a credit card bill, pay as much as you can at that moment. However, make a copy of the payment part of the bill. In fact, make several copies. Then when you get a little more money, write another check and send it in. Yes, it is a little more trouble and will cost you for additional envelopes, some stamps, and the cost of the copies. But it's worth the fifty cents to make even a ten- or twenty-dollar payment on your account. I have made two and three payments a month on a bill because I found I had an extra twenty dollars that wasn't obligated. So I obligated it before something else could come along. You will be chipping away at your debt, and you won't be tempted to spend the money on something else. Use all available income to pay down your debts.

Trevon!

✓ Don't think you can borrow your way out of debt.

Beware the temptation to borrow money to pay off debt. We have all been tempted by the debt consolidation home equity loans and on rare occasions those make sense. When you do it, you are reducing the interest on the amount owed: a good thing. But unless you can rein yourself in and not incur more unsecured credit card debt, then you are going to end up right where you are again: clearly a bad thing. Statistics say that about half of the people who use home equity to consolidate their debts end up right back where they were before they did the loan consolidation. They max their credit cards out again *and* have a home equity loan on top of it. You are probably better off just keeping your debts the way they are and paying them off as quickly as you can.

Don't borrow from family or friends. ✓

Friends, family, and funds should never be mixed. You might be able to pay off a bill, but you will probably end up losing a friend or causing resentment in your family. Even if they offer, my advice is to say no. You made the mess; it's up to you to fix it. In the long run you will be glad you did it alone.

Bankruptcy is rarely your best option and it should never be your first option.

I just watched a television commercial with a smiling bankruptcy attorney saying, "If you have too many bills and not enough money to go around, bankruptcy is your answer." I can tell you, that is an out-and-out lie. Bankruptcy is *an* answer. It might even be *the* answer. But it should not be your *first* answer.

Advertisements like that sucker people in because they offer an easy way out. People always want an easy way out. Let me tell you from firsthand experience that bankruptcy is not an easy way out. Bankruptcy may appear to be a quick fix, but it is actually rarely any kind of fix. In fact, I saw one study stating that as many as half the people who declare bankruptcy do so more than once, proving that bankruptcy didn't really solve anything for them. Their habits didn't change and they ended up in the same mess again. Bankruptcy doesn't alter personal behavior. Until you start to act differently by spending less, earning more, and saving, you are doomed to repeat the behavior that created the problem.

I know that people in horrible financial situations can become desperate. I know that bankruptcy can seem like your only option. I am aware that our society is full of people who are nothing but a bankruptcy looking for a place to happen. But do anything you can to avoid filing for bankruptcy.

"But, Larry, you did it."

Believe me, no one will ever let me forget that I did it. It's been nearly twenty years, and every time I want to buy a house or do anything on credit, they are quick to remind me. You will be told that a bankruptcy will eventually go away. Officially, at some point it won't count. But unofficially it will bite you in the ass for the rest of your life.

My personal bankruptcy was the result of a business bankruptcy. I was the president and minority stockholder of a small business. I willingly signed my name on the bank loans and tax forms, making personal guarantees for money the company could not pay back. The company went bankrupt for many reasons, not the least of which was my own stupidity. I made many of the mistakes and I'll take responsibility for them and accept the consequences. I went down shortly after the company went down. But at least when I went down, it wasn't because I couldn't stop shopping at the mall!

If you can avoid this last-ditch solution by reducing expenses and earning more money, you owe it to yourself to do so. In the next chapter, I'll show you how small changes add up to more money than you think.

CHAPTER FIVE

HOW TO CUT YOUR EXPENSES AND INCREASE YOUR INCOME

The only way to get more is to give more.

While it may sound strange, that is how it works. You give and *then* you get. But first you give. Then you get. Not the other way around. Lots of employees go to their bosses and say, "If you give me more money, then I'll give you more work." What their bosses should be saying is, "If you will give me more work, then I'll give you more money." This principle works in every area of life. You can't get more time to spend with your family until you give up the time you are spending doing something else. You can't get healthier until you give up what is making you unhealthy. And you can't get ahead until you are willing to give up the things that are keeping you broke.

WHAT ARE YOU WILLING TO GIVE UP?

Are you willing to give up some of your television time? Family time? Sleep? Clothes? Eating out? Shopping? Your car? Golf? Friends?

Tell me exactly what you think you could give up to either work more or learn more—anything absolutely nonessential.

MY LIST OF THINGS I AM WILLING TO GIVE UP:

_____

_____

_____

_____

_____

_____

_____

_____

_____

_____

_____

_____

_____

_____

_____

EVERYTHING COUNTS.

Don't think something is too insignificant to make a difference. Everything in your life either moves you closer or farther away from where you want to be. *Nothing is neutral.* No conversation, decision, or action. Every book, magazine, and television show moves you closer to or farther from your goal. Every friend you have moves you closer to your goals or farther away from your goals. Let's look at the things you should give up to move you closer to your goal of getting ahead financially.

Give up cable television. ✓

Cable television rates typically run around $100 per month. Twelve hundred bucks a year would go a long way toward reducing your debt, wouldn't it? Disconnect. You can do it!

I know, I know; how will you ever survive without HBO? You will. I told a guy on *Big Spender* that he had to give up cable television and he went ballistic on me. He said that was the step too far. I guess he thought working was too much to ask, too, because he didn't have a job. He had cable television but he didn't have a job. He got mad and screamed at me, "I heard you were once broke. What did you do?" I told him I sold blood to make my house payment and all I was doing was asking him to give up cable, so he needed to shut the hell up. He did.

Get some rabbit ears and watch whatever you can get. Or give up television altogether. A woman on *Big Spender* was so upset her television was gone that she screamed and cried about it. After a month of doing without it, she told me she didn't even want it back. She and her family were reading together and playing games and going for walks and having conversations. Their family was closer because the television was gone.

Get a cheaper car.

I worked with a man whose net take-home was $1,800 per month. His car payment was over $900 per month. He actually thought that was pretty good; just a month before, his car payment had been $1,200, and his fiancée talked him into getting a slightly cheaper car. My suggestion to him was to do whatever it took to get a $200-per-month car payment. I knew he was upside down in his car loan, and I didn't really care if he had to drive his $200-per-month car for the next fifteen years . . . he needed the cash flow to pay his other bills. I don't care who you are—to spend 50 percent of your income on a car is stupid. It took visiting nine dealerships before he could find someone who was able to help him. He ended up financing the cheaper car and the leftovers of the too-expensive-for-him car he had traded in. And he increased the length of time he had to make payments. Some might say that was a stupid move. I disagree. It gave him back $500 a month that he desperately needed. He was then able to pay off credit cards that had a 30 percent interest rate. He was able to play catch-up with the rest of his obligations.

Suck it up and trade in that expensive car you don't have the money to pay for, and get something that fits your budget. You are not your car. Get past the whole status symbol stupidity and realize that when you are in trouble, you don't need a status symbol; you need transportation.

Move.

I know this is a big step, but it is sometimes necessary. Lenders have been way too eager to loan people money to buy houses, and now those people can't afford their houses any longer. People have taken out interest-only loans and now their principal is about to kick in and they simply don't have the money. If that describes you, sell the house and move. Chances are you couldn't afford the house when you bought it; if you took out an interest-only loan, that was a clue! So cut your losses, learn your lesson, and move on. Or maybe you took out an adjustable-rate mortgage (ARM) that is now about to adjust, and you know there is no way you can make your new, higher payment. You don't want your house to be foreclosed, so sell while you still have a chance. You might not make much (if any) money if the market is depressed. You might even lose some money. Too bad. Sit down with a real estate professional and talk to your mortgage company and figure out the best step for you to take. By the way, when I say real estate professional, I mean someone who does more than list houses and complete the paperwork. I am talking about someone who has been in the market a while and has friends in the lending industry who can work with you to get you out of your mess.

If you rent, don't even think about this one; just find a cheaper place to live. Then move. Hard? Yes. Inconvenient? Of course. Necessary? Without a doubt.

✓ Give up your high-speed Internet connection.

Sorry. If you are scraping by and barely paying your bills, it's back to dial-up for you. And please don't tell me that you need it. Unless you make your living on the Internet, you don't need it. It is not a necessity. You just enjoy it. You get a kick out of it. It's entertaining. So is a book. Enjoy the Internet at a slower speed until you can easily pay for it.

Get rid of your home phone.

I know I just told you to rely on dial-up for your Internet connection, but you may be in such dire straits that even this is a bad idea. Keep your cell phone and dump your home phone.

Get a new cell phone plan.

Cut back on your minutes. Do whatever it takes to make your monthly expense lower. You don't need to download music videos on your phone. You don't need to answer e-mail on your phone. You only need to make necessary phone calls—especially those long-distance calls that you may currently be making on your home phone line at an extra cost. Your first necessary phone call is to your cell phone provider to cut back on your plan.

Cut your insurance expense.

Call your agent. Raise the deductible. Change your coverage. Do what it takes to lower your payment. This is for homeowners, auto, and health insurance. Change them all—keep your coverage, but do what you can to lower the costs.

Stop eating out.

I have already covered this one, but I want to say it again. It seems that one of the major reasons people don't have enough money to pay their bills is because they eat out too much. Why is there never enough money to pay the rent or make the car payment but always enough for a Big Mac? Don't tell me it is for the sake of convenience. Fast-food restaurants are rarely fast and it is never convenient to wait in line just to buy fake food that is going to shorten your life.

Stop going out.

You don't have the money to meet your buddies for a happy-hour drink after work. So don't. You don't have the money to meet your friends for golf or for lunch. You don't have the extra money to go to the movies. You don't even have the money to rent a movie. So don't do these things. You don't have the money for a lottery ticket. Chances are pretty good you aren't going to win anyway. You don't have the money for any nonessential spending right now. Someday you will, but for now you don't. It's time to pay the piper for your past mistakes. (By the way, *piper* is code for MasterCard, Visa, American Express, and Discover Card.)

Give up the salon.

Learn to color your own hair and do your own nails. It may not look as good, but you need that money for other things. And forget tanning salons and spas completely. That's an unnecessary expense.

There have been some women on my TV show who flat out refused this suggestion. That's fine. Don't do it and keep living on money you don't have or that you owe someone else. Which would make you feel better, a manicure or a payment on your debts? Until you can answer, "Paying a debt," you aren't ready to get ahead.

Drop the gym membership.

You aren't using it anyway, so save the money. There is plenty you can do to stay healthy at home without going to the gym. I believe in gyms. I believe in getting healthy and staying healthy, but it's a luxury you can live without while you are playing catch-up with your money. Walk. Run. Lift your kids. Go to the park with your kids. Get mad at me over this one all you want. But it is rare that a truly physically fit person who really uses a gym membership gets ticked off over this advice. It's always the fat folks who get mad about giving up their membership, even though they haven't waddled through the door of their gym in months. Give it up, go for a walk, and use the money to pay off your debts.

"But I have a contract." I hear that a lot. Talk to the gym manager. Explain your situation. Don't worry about embarrassing yourself; for all you know, the manager may be in the same shape you are. Just tell him that you can't pay for the membership any longer and you need a way out of it. Work something out.

Stop smoking.

At $4 per pack, a one-pack-a-day habit is $1,460 per year. If you live long enough to smoke for forty years, that is $58,400. If you made a yearly contribution of $1,460 to a tax-deferred savings account such as an IRA or 401(k), with a projected interest rate of 8 percent compounded annually, you could have over $400,000 for retirement or your children's future or to enjoy in your old age.

Here is the question, Smoker. Is it worth it? What is more important: your kid's financial future or your cigarette? On top of the stupidity of the expense, you are killing yourself. Quit and spend the money on your financial security, not on dying early.

WHAT WILL YOU DO WITH YOUR TIME?
MAKE A PLAN!

Now that you know some things you should give up and even have a list of things you are willing to give up, you have to have something there to replace those items. If you don't have things ready to fill in the holes you have just created, you might fill them in with more things that do you little or no good. Have your stack of self-improvement books ready to go so when you turn the television off, you will be ready to replace your television time with some reading time. If you are going to give up eating out, you'd better have some groceries ready to go that you can prepare. If you give up going to the mall, what will you do instead? Go to the library? Exercise? What? Remember the law of physics that says nature abhors a vacuum. If you create a space in your life, something will show up to fill it in. You are in charge of what fills in the space you have created.

"But, Larry, this is all such a sacrifice!"

Okay, then don't do it. Don't sacrifice your lifestyle and just keep living the way you are right now. It's up to you.

> In order to have what you have never had
> and get something you have never gotten,
> you have to do something you have never done.

HOW TO MAKE MONEY.

> You can't *make* money.
> You can only *earn* money.

Never again say, "I need to make more money." You aren't the Treasury Department and you don't get to print it up when you need it. You have to earn it. That's always where the money comes from. Instead say, "I need to earn more money."

Earn more money.

Remember I told you there were only two ways to get ahead: reduce expenses or increase income. So far, I've only talked about reducing expenses, but now it's time to address increasing income. This probably means getting a second job. Sometimes it takes one job to get by and another job to get ahead.

"What? A second job? Don't you want me to have a life?"

Actually, that is exactly what I want for you. I want you to have a life where you aren't living paycheck to paycheck. A future that isn't full of worries and concerns over how to pay your bills. A real life. The life you want. And if it means you have to get a second job to make that happen, then suck it up.

When I was broke and struggling I tied macramé, trimmed trees, painted houses, swept floors, and even sold blood. You do what it takes when you have to. I'm not above doing what it takes. Even as a rich guy, I always look for ways to make extra money. Just in the last few years I have flipped houses and owned a mobile cigar company.

I'm always amazed at capable men and women who are unemployed and yet won't take a job sacking groceries because it is beneath them. If I have bills to pay and groceries to buy and kids to clothe, then nothing is beneath me. No honest job is below my level.

Recently I was sitting with my wife at a great outdoor restaurant in San Diego's Gaslamp Quarter when a guy came by and started digging in the trash can. A lot of things jumped into my mind: He's homeless and looking for something to eat, he's looking for a cigarette or a half-full can of beer, his predicament is sad, it's his own fault—all of that and more ran through my mind in one second as I watched him scour through the trash can. Then I saw that he was actually pulling out plastic soda bottles and aluminum cans and sticking them in a couple of big bags he had. After a few seconds he ran to the next trash can . . . yep, he ran. He was digging out stuff that could be recycled and he was moving as fast as he could to get as much as he could—probably so he could make it to the place where he'd cash it all in before they closed. This guy had a job. It probably wasn't the job he had always wanted, or even wanted now, but it was what was available to him and he was doing it. He was working. I admired this guy. He wasn't begging or griping (at least not to me); he was hustling along the sidewalk doing what he could that day to make a buck. Could he do more? Probably. Couldn't we all? Absolutely. I have no idea what this guy's story was. He could have been homeless and this was how he got money to eat. This could also have been a second job or a third job. What matters is that here was a guy who was willing to do something most people wouldn't do. Are you?

Are you willing to take on an extra job to pay off your bills earlier? If you aren't willing to do whatever it takes to get ahead, then you don't deserve to get ahead.

Most people don't want to *earn* more money . . . they just want to *have* more. I guess the Money Fairy is supposed to slip into your bank account at night and deposit money. Even the Tooth Fairy expects you to leave a tooth behind in exchange for the money. You give up the tooth; the Tooth Fairy gives up a little coinage. That is how the

Money Fairy works too: You give up a little work and the Money Fairy shows up with a little money.

Everyone can do something. Everyone has a skill that can be marketed. Everyone can do more than they are doing. You might not like it, but it can still be done. While there is never a shortage of ways to earn money, there is a shortage of willingness to do whatever it takes to earn money.

> Life is not made up of the haves and the have-nots—but instead of the wills and the will-nots.

By the way . . . and this is a BIG by the way:

Earning more is not a license to spend more. It does no good to go out and make an extra $500 a month if you are going to spend an extra $600 a month. I worked with a woman who got a second job to pay for her shopping habit. But her habit was to spend more than she earned and her habit didn't change. So the second job only allowed her to overspend at a higher income level. The extra income you earn goes toward reducing your debts so you can save and give and live without the stress and worry that comes from overspending. Sometimes, though, an extra job may not be enough.

Sell stuff.

If you are in desperate need of cash to pay your obligations, then sell your stuff. When I filed for bankruptcy and was in serious financial trouble, I sold everything. My wife and I agreed that we wouldn't sell our wedding rings—but *everything else* was fair game. I even sold our sofa and living room chairs. We sat on the floor. I hated it. It was humiliating. But I did it. I had to. I needed the cash to pay my commitments. My commitments meant more to me than my stuff.

Begin by selling your toys. It's not playtime any longer—it's time to save your ass. Get rid of the boat, the motorcycle, the RV, the four-wheelers, the gym equipment I bet you don't use anyway, the fishing equipment, the hunting equipment, the golf clubs, the Jet Skis, and the bicycles. "But, Larry, those are my hobbies. I love that stuff." Too bad. Bye-bye. You can buy new stuff once your bills are paid off and you're in a better place financially.

Next, go to your closet. Go to the bad end of your closet. (Guys, you didn't even know you had a bad end in your closet, did you? This is the stuff you don't wear, can't wear, and wouldn't wear on a bet.) Pull everything out and get all of it ready for a yard sale or the consignment shop.

Then take a good look at your furniture. Do you really need that chair? Be tough on yourself . . . you have bills to pay!

Think garage sale, yard sale, consignment shops, pawnshops, eBay, and craigslist.com. These are just places to start. Post your stuff on bulletin boards at work. Get creative and get selling!

I know it is hard to get rid of the things you have. You like your stuff. We all do. But this is a time to like getting out of debt more than you like the things you own. It's just stuff! Stop being so attached—it's unhealthy. Especially if you're holding on to it as a symbol of prosperity that doesn't reflect the reality of your situation.

MY PERSONAL SYMBOL OF PROSPERITY.

When I started making some real money, I wanted to reward myself. I had worked my ass off to get rich, so I decided to buy a gorgeous little Porsche Carrera convertible. Did I need it? Nope. But rewards are rarely about need; they are almost always about want. I wanted it, so I bought it. Holy crap, it was a hot little car. Did I have any problem buying it? Not at all. I could afford it. If you find yourself in the same position, I suggest you do the same thing. It was a symbol of my prosperity. When you do well, you want a reward and I think you should have it.

Here is the problem with a Porsche: It's not the most practical car in the world. Not that you buy it to be practical, you buy it because you can and because it says PORSCHE on the back end. Golf clubs, bulldogs, groceries, and suitcases don't fit in a Porsche very well. Neither does anything else except the driver and a small friend. While I loved my Porsche and enjoyed driving it, I bought other cars—three other cars. So my wife and I had a total of four cars for the two of us to drive. And I travel most of the time. My symbol of prosperity had officially become a symbol of excess. A little excess isn't necessarily a bad thing if you can afford it—and I could. I just liked knowing I could afford to own an amazing car whether I ever drove it or not. Does that make sense? Sure it does . . . for a while.

Then I stopped driving it almost completely. In fact, in two years I drove it fewer than seven hundred miles. I'll do the calculation for you: That's less than thirty miles per month! A set of tires rotted on it while it sat in my garage. I had to keep it plugged in all the time just so it would start, because the battery kept dying due to lack of use. My wife tried to get me to sell it. I refused. But one day, after replacing the tires and the battery and having to walk around it every day to get to my three other cars, I realized that my symbol of prosperity had gone beyond my symbol of excess to become a symbol of my stupidity. So I sold it. I had nothing to prove to myself or to anyone else any longer. I didn't need a reminder that I was doing well. Now I drive a pickup truck and don't give a damn what anyone thinks about it. See? Still a redneck at heart!

One time there was a woman on my show who had nearly $20,000 worth of shoes. She loved her shoes. But based on her income and her other bills, she simply couldn't afford to support that kind of shoe habit. I told her she needed to sell most of her shoes to pay her bills. She flatly refused. Her brother offered to pay her the full retail amount of her shoes so she could pay off her debts. Again, she refused. Her shoes made the move from symbols of prosperity and excess to symbols of stupidity.

Another woman on the show had over two hundred DVDs—many unopened. She just liked having them. I told her to sell them to pay her bills, which were in collection! She sold fifteen. She thought the others were "collectors' items." DVDs are never collectors' items. (By the way, I have noticed from working with people who have real money issues that most have huge DVD collections. So if you see yourself getting too many, you might want to stop and think about it!)

Are you really much different from these two women or me? Don't you have things that have made the transition from a symbol of prosperity to a symbol of excess to a symbol of stupidity? I had a Porsche. For one lady it was shoes. For another it was DVDs. What is it with you?

Write it down:

_____

_____

_____

_____

Now make a list of all the other stuff you can sell. When you finish the list, do a walk through the house and make your list longer. Reality check: I know you will probably only get about 10 cents on the dollar for the stuff. You will find yourself saying things like, "I paid $400 for this and now I can only get $40." That's how it works. Sorry. The point is that you need that $40 to pay a bill. You also need a fresh, clean start. Get rid of the stuff that is weighing you down. Unclutter your life by ridding yourself of useless items. In doing so, you will make space for new habits and ways of thinking that will get you ahead.

STUFF I COULD SELL RIGHT NOW:

CHAPTER SIX

THE STUFF MOST PEOPLE OVERLOOK

I probably haven't surprised you with any-thing I've suggested up to this point. This stuff is mostly just common sense. And if you watch television, and I would lay odds you watch a lot of it, then you may have heard most of the ideas I have offered up to this point many times. You just haven't acted on them. This chapter will probably have some stuff you haven't heard before—stuff that may surprise you or even seem trivial and insignificant. Yet it is this stuff that can make the difference between getting by and getting ahead.

Read on for changes you can make that will have a tremendous impact on your financial future. If you do these things, I guarantee you will get ahead!

CHANGE CHECKING ACCOUNTS.

Many banks have checking accounts that round up the amount of the check you write and put the odd cents in a savings account. If you write a check for $18.37, then 63 cents will go into a savings account. You will be amazed how quickly this adds up.

TAXES. PAY THEM.

Like everyone, I gripe a bit when it comes to paying my taxes. But when I find myself whining about taxes, I remember a time when I didn't have to pay taxes. Can you imagine that? No taxes. I definitely don't want a year like that ever again. Know why? I didn't make any money! I just try to remind myself that I enjoy the things my taxes pay for. I like roads to drive on and police and fire protection. I'm not wild about *all* the things my taxes pay for. But there are times when you take the bad along with the good, and paying taxes is one of those times.

GET A GOOD BANKER.

Know your banker by name. Make sure your banker knows you by name. Go into your local branch and meet someone. Explain who you are and what you would like to do. It will be hard. I still have a problem with this one because people at banks come and go, and for the most part don't care about you or your money. Keep asking until you find someone who does. Remember, they need your business. Even if you are a bad customer, they make money on your bounced-check charges.

PICK UP THE PENNY.

A penny is interest on one dollar for one month. Pick it up and put it in your pocket. I pick up at least one every day. I have a big jar that I fill up every year with change I have picked up off the street. Picking up the penny is a reminder to me that money is important. It is also proof that money is always flowing into your life; you just have to pay attention and be willing to pick it up. I watch people walk right past pennies on the street. Maybe they don't see them. I see them all. I have trained myself to spot money wherever it presents itself. I even have a little mantra that I have said for the past twenty years: "Money comes to me from all directions." It does. It does for you, too. You just haven't trained yourself to recognize that, and you might not be willing to take the steps to take advantage of the situation. Or maybe you think the amount is too insignificant. No amount of money is insignificant. It adds up—even a penny at a time.

I know that picking up a penny won't make me rich.

But after picking it up, I will have more money than I had before I picked it up, and that is the overall direction I want to be moving in at all times.

When I was a little boy, my dad once asked me, "If I hired you to go to work for me and I agreed to double your salary every day you worked for me, but the first day your salary would only be a penny—day two it would be two pennies, day three only four pennies, and so on— would you take the job?"

As a small child I said, "No! No way I would work for so little! I'm worth more than a few pennies." Then my dad explained to me how quickly I would be rich if I agreed to take the job. He got a sheet of paper and told me to figure it out. I did. This is what I came up with:

Day 1...... $0.01	Day 11.... $10.24	Day 21.... $10,485.76
Day 2...... $0.02	Day 12.... $20.48	Day 22.... $20,971.52
Day 3..... $0.04	Day 13... $40.96	Day 23.... $41,943.04
Day 4...... $0.08	Day 14.... $81.92	Day 24.... $83,886.08
Day 5..... $0.16	Day 15.... $163.84	Day 25.... $167,772.16
Day 6...... $0.32	Day 16.... $327.68	Day 26.... $335,544.32
Day 7..... $0.64	Day 17... $655.36	Day 27.... $671,088.64
Day 8...... $1.28	Day 18.... $1,310.72	Day 28.... $1,342,177.28
Day 9...... $2.56	Day 19.... $2,621.44	Day 29.... $2,684,354.56
Day 10.... $5.12	Day 20.... $5,242.88	Day 30.... $5,368,709.12

The amazing thing to me as a child and even now is the speed at which money multiplies. So while it won't happen quite this fast in real life, remember that even a meager start in saving and paying your way out of debt will build very quickly. (In the meantime, if someone makes you this offer, take it!)

CARRY CASH. ✔

The best thing about cash is that when it is gone, it's gone. The worst thing about cash is that when it's gone, it's gone! With a credit card you can slide right past your limit. Even with a debit card, your bank will probably allow you to slide right past zero and then charge you a hefty amount for doing it. Not so with cash.

This is what you should do. Is your budget $200 a month for groceries? Then get an envelope and write GROCERIES on it. When you get paid, cash your check and put $200 cash in the envelope. When you go to the grocery store, you use this envelope and only this envelope to pay for your groceries. When the $200 is gone, you stop buying groceries and you stop eating. Repeat this process with every cash item on your budget. Envelopes full of cash are the way to go until you get a handle on your spending.

SAVE YOUR CHANGE. ✔

When I buy something and pay cash, I never use change. I always break a dollar and get the change back. When

I get home, I dump that change in a one-gallon milk bottle that I keep in my closet. A one-gallon jar holds about $400 worth of change. Usually I use it to buy something cool that I want. In the old days of less money, I would pay a bill with it. Try my suggestion. Just break a dollar bill to pay for things and save the change. You won't miss it and when your jar is full, you will be able to do something significant.

SHOP WITH A LIST AND A BUDGET.

Most purchases are unplanned and not budgeted for. This has to stop. Make a list of what you need and how much you have to spend on it. Stick to the list. Don't vary from the list for any reason. When you get to the checkout, if you pull something out of your basket that wasn't on the list, tell the cashier to set it aside because you have changed your mind. This isn't a game—this is war. Have the discipline to win the war by sticking to your list and your budget. (More on making that budget in Chapter 7!)

BUILD A CUSHION. SAVE!

Save for an emergency. Some financial advisors say you should have six months' worth of living expenses in your savings account. That won't happen for most people. I say shoot for one month's worth of living expenses as a bare minimum. Put it away and don't touch it for any reason.

By the way, a credit card is not your first source of emergency funds. Cash is the first source. Just because you have a "clean" credit card, it doesn't mean you are ready for an emergency.

And don't think you are emergency immune. You aren't. People get laid off. Companies go out of business. Medical emergencies happen. Elderly parents get sick and you have to step in to take care of them. Bad stuff does happen to good people. I understand that. Be prepared.

I filmed a television show with a couple who had no money, no jobs, lots of bills, and no plan for things to get better. They were resistant to every suggestion I made, yet they agreed to follow my plan for thirty days. Part of my plan was to stash just $200 away as an emergency fund. Begrudgingly, they did it. They would rather have spent it on fun stuff but they did as I asked. Before I could go back to do my follow-up with them to see how their month had gone, his father had a heart attack and had to be hospitalized. Luckily, he had the money—that $200 emergency fund—to fly back and see his father. This guy didn't much like me or my ideas for his money . . . until then. When we wrapped the show, his tearful confession was that without that $200 he would not have been able to see his father. I originally had no hope for this couple and their future—yet that event turned them around and they are now doing great.

Don't wait for an emergency to happen to find out you need an emergency fund. Prepare now. Open a savings account just for this purpose and stash a few bucks in it at every opportunity. This is not a vacation fund or fun fund. This money is to be used when it hits the fan and you need help.

FORGET COUPONS.

I know this is blasphemy to a lot of people. However, using coupons is not always about being frugal. Sometimes it is about being cheap. The amount of time it took you to scour the paper for coupons could have been spent getting smarter or earning more money.

When I want something and it happens to be offered at a discount, or I happen upon a coupon that allows me to buy exactly what I want cheaper, then I take advantage of the coupon or the discount. Not to get what you want at a lower price when you can is stupid.

However, this is not what I am talking about. I am talking about people who alter what they want based on the discount or the coupon.

I know people who decide where they want to eat based on their stack of coupons. You want Chinese food for dinner, but you have a coupon for pizza so you wind up eating pizza just because of the coupon. If you do this, you are being cheap. You are compromising your desires and settling for less than you deserve. You are letting discounts determine your life and have allowed yourself to become the victim of a stupid coupon. Get in control. Live your life the way you want to live it. Don't have the money to do that? Remind yourself that your condition is your own damn fault and then commit and constantly recommit yourself to having the money to live any way you want to live.

DON'T BUY IN BULK.

I love Sam's and Costco. I love walking the aisles and am constantly amazed at the bargains you can get there. You really can save money at the warehouse clubs. But be careful! Things that look like a bargain, while being cheaper than you would normally pay, don't always end up being a bargain. Because things are so much cheaper per item, people tend to buy more than they need and end up spending more than they have to. I don't care if it is the buy of the century, no one needs a four-pack of 64-ounce bottles of ketchup. Unless it is something that can be consumed quickly, completely, and constantly, like toilet paper, then you are paying too much when you buy bulk quantities.

READ.

How many self-help books, business books, or biographies have you read in the last year? Okay, let's widen the search even more. How many books of any kind have you read in the last year?

It is an easy question that doesn't require a story or any excuses—it just requires a number. So what is the number? Take the next step. Write down the names of the self-help books, business books, or biographies you have read in the past twelve months.

MY LIST OF BOOKS:

You're Broke Because You Want to Be

Nothing on your list? Then you aren't serious about improving your life. You aren't taking action on becoming more prosperous. You have to study in order to achieve what you want. Your situation, especially your financial situation, will improve right after *you* improve.

Interesting factoid: A study by the U.S. government found that 46–51 percent of U.S. adults read and write so poorly that they earn significantly below poverty level wages.

> **Everything in life gets better when you get better, and nothing in life gets better until you get better.**

"But there isn't enough time to read!!!"

Sure there is. The average welfare recipient has the same amount of time every day as the average billionaire. It's not how much time you have; it's how you choose to spend the time.

I've read nearly four thousand books in the past twenty years. I read them when I was broke and I read them now that I'm rich. But especially when I was broke. I was searching to find out from every source possible how to live a better life. If your life isn't what you want it to be in any area, then you should be doing the same thing. When something is important to you, you find the time.

The good news is that you are now reading a book.

But this is only one book. I'll admit that it is a great book, but you can't stop after one great book. You need to search for more great books. Read some great books about the philosophy of wealth. Here are a few I especially like:

Think and Grow Rich, by Napoleon Hill
Manifest Your Destiny, by Dr. Wayne W. Dyer
Creating Affluence, by Deepak Chopra
You Were Born Rich, by Bob Proctor
*Why You're Dumb, Sick & Broke . . . and How to Get
    Smart, Healthy & Rich!*, by Randy Gage

After you've read about the philosophy of being wealthy it's time to get some very practical advice about getting rich. I can help get you from broke to breaking even so you will have some money to start building wealth and getting rich, but the next step is up to you. To take it to the next level, try these books:

Rich Dad, Poor Dad, by Robert T. Kiyosaki
Start Late, Finish Rich, by David Bach
Never Eat Alone, by Keith Ferrazzi
The Millionaire Zone, by Jennifer Openshaw
Go Put Your Strengths to Work, by Marcus
    Buckingham

And for overall success in life and business, definitely read anything by Larry Winget, especially *It's Called*

Work for a Reason! Your Success Is Your Own Damn Fault and *Shut Up, Stop Whining & Get a Life*

Reading increases your worth—ultimately your net worth—but also your worth to others. The more you know, the more you are worth. The more you are worth, the more you will earn. As success philosopher Jim Rohn says, "If you knew better, you would do better."

CHANGE YOUR LANGUAGE.

If you constantly think like you are broke, talk like you are broke, and do the things a broke person does, then you will be broke. This is the type of language I want you to change:

"I can't afford . . ."

If you say that you can't afford something, you will *never* be able to afford it. Saying "I can't afford" makes you a victim. The price of things does not dictate whether you can have them or not. That isn't the case and we both know it. You are in control. So talk like you are in control. Instead say, "I don't choose to spend the money I have right now on that." Even if you don't have the money! This statement is a reminder that spending is a choice. Your entire life is about choices. You control the choices you make. That is a position of power, not victimhood.

Speaking of having control over your choices . . .

LOSE WEIGHT AND CLEAN UP YOUR HOUSE.

If your spending is out of control, then chances are very good that other parts of your life are out of control. Let me give you my observations. These are broad, sweeping statements, and there are exceptions—but I have found that . . .

People who are out of control with their spending are usually out of control with their eating. People who spend big usually eat big.

People who are out of control with their spending are usually out of control in their relationships.

People who are out of control with their spending are usually out of control when it comes to keeping their houses and cars clean.

A lack of personal discipline in one area nearly always shows up in other areas. Watch the shows on television about cleaning up and reorganizing a room in a house. The ones where a camera crew goes into a room they can't even walk through. Sometimes there is stuff that is stacked waist deep in a bedroom with only a small trail to a bed that is covered in crap. I guarantee you those people have money problems. And sorry, but many of them are also overweight.

I can walk through your house and tell you what your

checkbook looks like. Do it yourself right now. Take a quick look around your house. Is it tidy? Clean? Are your closets and drawers organized? Are the dishes clean and put away? If so, it is likely that you have a neat, tidy system for keeping track of your money.

Or do you have piles of dirty clothes on the floor? Are *all* of your drawers junk drawers? Is the garage a disaster? If this is the case, I am guessing you have no idea how much money you have or who you owe.

When you get control over one area of your life, then the other areas start to come together. Get everything going for you that you can by fixing the things you control in each area of your life.

EAT LESS.

One of the best ways to lose weight *and* save some money would be to simply eat less.

I worked with a couple who spent $20,000 a year eating out and still spent $18,000 a year on groceries. Two people! That $38,000 was equivalent to one of their salaries. Of course I cut all eating-out from their budget, but I also decreased the amount they were spending on groceries. It was just too much.

When making a budget, I always leave people $50 per person per week in grocery money. Any person can have plenty to eat on that much money. I'm talking about a healthy diet. People who argue that it can't be done are not eating sensibly. They are buying cookies and prepared foods that cost a lot and eat up their food budget. I took one woman to the grocery store to watch her shop the way she normally did for her husband and four-year-old son. She bought prepared meals (we used to call them TV dinners) for almost every meal. She bought bags of cookies and sugar-laden cereals, soda, candy, and chips. Her basket was full and yet she didn't have any real food in it. She even bought prepared mashed potatoes. What? I asked her if she couldn't boil her own potatoes and mash them herself, and she told me she wasn't Betty Crocker. Imagine her displeasure when I made her put it all back and shop with only the one hundred dollar bill I gave her. I walked her through the store, buying meat, chicken, fish, vegetables, whole-grain breads and cereal, and lots of fruit. I helped her fill her basket with real food that would last for more than a week and when we went to the checkout line, she still had money left over. Yes, she and her husband would have to cook it. No, it wouldn't keep for weeks. Yes, it was less food than they were used to eating. But that was a good thing. They were both overweight, so they were actually doing both their budget and their waistlines a huge favor.

Take a hard look at your food budget. I know you probably don't have a food budget, but you are going to have one from now on. How much do you spend on food every week? Decide to spend less. Use my $50-per-person-per-week plan. Buy healthier food, which costs less. Prepare it yourself, which costs nothing. The meals will be good for you, good for your family, and you might even enjoy doing it. Besides, if you are an average person in today's society you could easily afford to lose a few pounds.

TAKE A TOUGH LOOK AT YOUR FRIENDS.

In Randy Gage's book *Why You're Dumb, Sick & Broke . . . and How to Get Smart, Healthy & Rich*, he quotes one of our shared heroes, Jim Rohn, in saying that your income will be the average earnings of your five closest friends. I believe this to be true. That's why I try to surround myself with very rich people. Don't believe it? Let's try it right now. I want you to write down the names of your five closest friends and then write down how much money you figure they make and average it out. Don't pick up the phone and call them; you pretty much know how much money they make!

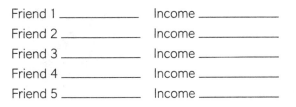

Friend 1 _____   Income _____

Friend 2 _____   Income _____

Friend 3 _____   Income _____

Friend 4 _____   Income _____

Friend 5 _____   Income _____

Add them all together and divide by five. What's the average?_____

The formula works, doesn't it? What's the message? You may want to upgrade your friends. Does that mean you have to dump your old friends? That probably isn't a totally bad idea! But at least try to develop new friends who embody the traits you would like to see more of in your own life.

Ask yourself these questions about your friends:

> What do you and your friends talk about? Do you make fun of rich people? Put other people down? Do you bitch and gripe and whine about work and how unfair life is?
> What books do your friends read? (If you answer this question with "Books?" that would be a clue.)
> What do your friends expect from you?
> What do your friends let you get by with?

If the answers to these questions are not ones you are particularly proud of, then you face the tough decision of keeping friends who are keeping you from your goals or choosing new friends who move you closer to your goals.

This is not easy, I know. But I can promise you, if it were a choice between my friends and the financial welfare of my family, I would dump my broke-ass friends in a heartbeat.

BE GENEROUS IN TIPPING AND BILL SPLITTING.

Want to know if someone is cheap? Have dinner with them and watch what happens when the bill comes. Anyone who starts saying things like, "But I only had water, so mine is two dollars less," is a cheap person. Divide the total bill by the number of people eating, pay up, and move on.

Lousy tippers are killing their chances at ever being prosperous. If you are less than generous with others, others will be less than generous with you.

GIVE AWAY SOME OF YOUR MONEY.

I know, I know. I tell you to stop all spending except on the necessities, to focus on your debt, and to save all you can, and now I am telling you to just give away your money. Doesn't make sense, does it? You are so right. It doesn't make any sense . . . except it works. When you willingly share part of what you have earned with others, then it magically comes back to you. I don't know why it works, but I know it works.

Proof that it works:

After my business failure and bankruptcy, I was broke. I stopped giving money to charity because I didn't feel like

I could afford to give any away. While most would think my actions justifiable, my parents had taught me that if you have *anything*, you should share it with those who have *nothing*.

One day as I sat in my office, I had an absolutely overwhelming urge to write a check and give away some money. I felt like I needed to give away $100. While that isn't a lot of money, at the time it seemed like a huge amount—especially since it was $100 more than I had given in a very long time. Plus, it seemed that I had so many bills and other obligations, Christmas was coming soon and I had two little boys to buy presents for, and I needed to spend my money on other things. Regardless, I couldn't shake this need to give. So I followed my gut and immediately wrote out a check for $100 to one of my favorite charities, stuck it in an envelope, addressed it, and put a stamp on it. I became so afraid that I would back out on sending it that I got in my car and took it immediately to the post office and dropped it in the outgoing mail. I felt instant relief about doing it, although I had no idea how to tell my wife what I had done. She was the one trying to stretch our small amount of money to cover our large amount of bills every month, and a hundred dollars less in the account was not going to be easy to explain.

That night at my home, my doorbell rang. It was my attorney. Since most attorneys don't make house calls, I wondered what in the world he could want that was so important he would come to my house at night. I invited him in. He told me that he had just had someone call him to forgive a huge debt that he owed in his business and he wanted to pass his good fortune along by forgiving some of his debtors. He then handed me a statement of my account and told me that it had been forgiven and to have a nice evening. As I looked, dumbfounded, at my bill, I noticed that the balance on my account had been $100.

Some might say that is an interesting coincidence. And maybe that's all it is. But for both my wife and me, it was a lesson to never stop giving, no matter what your circumstances. It is just the right thing to do.

I don't often quote preachers but coming from Tulsa, Oklahoma, makes you very familiar with Oral Roberts and his ministry. I don't care what anyone thinks of him; that isn't my point. Years ago I read something he said that forever changed the way I think about giving: "A rejected opportunity to give is a lost opportunity to receive."

Will that happen if you give? No guarantees from me. I have no clue whether it will happen to you or not. I just know that the best way to begin any money venture, whether it is an investment or getting out of debt, is to give away some money.

I personally believe in giving away 10 percent of your

money, but not for the religious reasons some people use. So I don't use the word *tithe*. (In fact, I don't want you to ever think about or use the word *tithe* again. The word just has too much religion associated with it.) When I hear the word *tithe* I think of a pompadour-haired preacher on television, wearing a turquoise suit and telling me that God needs my money and that if I will send it to the preacher, he will make sure God gets it. Personally, I don't think God needs or even wants your money. I don't think God gives a hoot about your silly 10 percent. You shouldn't give because you think God wants you to or because other people need it, though other people certainly do need it. You should give because you have faith you will have more money coming in. You need to attest to the fact that you can learn to live on the remaining 90 percent. You need to trust yourself to the point that you know more money is on the way even though you are giving some of what you have to people who need it even more than you do.

Money flows. Money comes to you and it goes from you. If you are unwilling to give your money away, you prove that you lack trust that money will ever come back to you. If your hand is gripped too tight to release what you have, then you won't be able to open up your hand to receive more.

Again, I don't care how broke you are, you can still figure out how to give something away. Do it.

Giving is also part of the obligation that comes

from having money. Yes, I said obligation. When you have money, you are obligated to share a portion of it with those who don't have money. Not the broke people of the world who can get off their butts and work to earn their own money but the poor people of the world who have little chance to do any better.

TUCK A BENJAMIN.

A Benjamin is a one hundred dollar bill. I like 'em. I like 'em a lot. I try to collect as many of them as I can. I always keep one folded and tucked down in the dark recesses of my wallet. You should too.

It will help you feel better about your situation. With a Benjamin in your pocket, you will think of yourself as a prosperous person. And you will never be broke. A prosperous person who isn't broke acts with confidence. Trust me, it will help. If you get caught in an emergency and are forced to use it, replace it as quickly as you can.

Can't do a hundred? Start with a twenty. Then move up to a fifty. Then one hundred. The hundred is the magic bill. No matter how rich you may find yourself someday, the face of Benjamin Franklin smiling at you will always make your day a little brighter.

BE THANKFUL FOR WHAT YOU HAVE.

"I don't have very much, so what do I have to be thankful for?"

You could have less, couldn't you? Sure you could. Remember that old saying "I felt sorry for the man who had no shoes, until I saw a man who had no feet." Things could be worse for you. Don't ever say anything stupid like, "Boy, things couldn't get any worse than this!" Believe me, if there is one thing I have learned about life, it is that things can always get worse! So even when things appear to be terrible for you, be thankful that they aren't worse. You have the talent and the ability to improve things. You can make things better. That alone is plenty to be thankful for. To remind yourself of all the good you have going for yourself in the midst of all the bad, I want you to make a list. Yes, another list!

"The more you are thankful for what you have, the more you will have to be thankful for."

—Zig Ziglar

WHAT I'M THANKFUL FOR:

_____

_____

_____

_____

_____

_____

_____

_____

_____

_____

> "A grateful mind is a great mind, which eventually attracts to itself great things."
>
> —Plato's _Laws_

FAMILY FINANCIAL FAUX PAS

I get hundreds of e-mails from people who are concerned about their family members who are in financial trouble. Some of these letters are desperate cries for help, clearly written out of both love for that person and the pain caused by watching them suffer. They tell me how they have tried everything to save their brother or daughter or other family member from financial ruin and yet nothing seems to work. Here is why nothing works: The family member in trouble doesn't want to change the situation. The sad truth is that you can't change it for him. You can't rescue someone who doesn't want to be rescued.

People who need help rarely appreciate the help. Most won't even accept the help. You can only help people when they want to be helped. Has your family member asked for help? I mean, more than just asking to borrow money to get out of a bind. Has she asked for help in changing how she lives so she won't get in a bind again? If she hasn't asked for that kind of help, chances are she doesn't really want to change her life. She doesn't want to stop being broke. She just wants to be bailed out when she has gone the step too far.

An additional problem in trying to rescue someone is that you perpetuate the idea in his mind that he is a victim. After all, you only rescue victims, right? You also confirm that same idea about him in your own mind, meaning that you will treat him like a victim. Stop treating others like victims. Instead, treat them like responsible individuals who have created their own messes and who have the ability to clean up their messes. You should help them clean up their messes if they want help and ask for help. But let them learn the value of self-respect by taking responsibility for their actions. Throw them the rope, but let them climb out of the hole on their own.

Since most of the requests I receive are from parents

who want to help their children, I know your role in teaching your kids about money is important.

Kids and money.

The only thing kids know about money is what you teach them. You set the example. Don't expect your kids to learn how to spend their money wisely if they have watched you piss yours away on stupid stuff. Your choices will become their choices. Every dime you spend shows them how to spend their money.

Kids should earn their money.

Give kids chores to do for pay. These should be special chores, not the chores that come with being a part of the family. As part of a family, they should automatically do things like help clear the table, empty the dishwasher (or even be the dishwasher), help with their own laundry, vacuum the house, carry out the trash, and pick up after themselves. This goes for both boys and girls. I don't agree with the notion of girl chores and boy chores. A boy can help in the kitchen and a girl can help in the garage. I am talking about chores that go above and beyond the normal stuff—maybe washing the car or mowing the lawn or cleaning out the gutters. It isn't my job to figure what the job is; it's your job. My point is that when kids earn their money, they learn to respect both the work and the money.

✓ "I want my kids to have better than I had."

We all do. It's normal. But it can easily be overdone. You don't do your kids a favor by buying them everything they want or everything you didn't have. I have dealt with many parents who thought they were showing their kids love by buying them everything they could dream of. I have seen a closet full of hundreds of outfits for a one-year-old baby. Clothes with the tags still on that she would never get to wear because she would outgrow them too fast. I have been in houses where you couldn't walk through any room in the house because of the toys—toys that had never been played with and never would be. In every situation the parents had not put aside one penny for their children's education. When I attacked them for their ridiculous spending, they tried to convince me that they did it out of love for their children.

I have dealt with parents who were about to have their houses foreclosed on and their cars repossessed, yet still had convinced themselves that buying hundreds of dollars worth of clothes and toys each month for their one-year-old was a good idea. They wanted to make sure she was happy. A one-year-old is happy when you hold her and hug her and feed her. You can give her a cardboard box to play with and she will be tickled pink.

Parents who spend their money only on things that have no future value are not showing love for their kids. What they are really doing is showing how uncaring and irresponsible they are. They are playing fast and loose with their children's future. They are robbing their kids of their education. In my opinion, this is a form of child abuse. Tough language, I know, but to steal your child's future is a serious offense, in my book.

Teach your kids about credit.

Show them your credit card statements and explain what interest rates mean. Tell them how a house that costs $300,000 doesn't really cost $300,000 when you pay for it over the next thirty years.

Advise them that they will be bombarded with credit card applications as soon as they reach eighteen years of age and teach them the pitfalls of credit card abuse. Don't let your kids be blindsided by the false promises of the good life that credit card companies advertise.

✓ When your kids get in financial trouble, help them. But not every time.

Let your kids suffer the pain of their decisions. That's how they will learn to make better decisions. Let them worry and feel remorse for their overspending. Let them suffer the embarrassment of receiving a collections call. Let them do without and let them pay some late charges. It's good for them. Really. Lessons not learned will be repeated. However, sometimes there may be a legitimate reason to help your kids.

When it comes to helping your kids with a money problem, you have to decide whether it is going to be a gift or whether you are making them a loan. Either way, make it clear which one it is. A gift is easier. That way you know going in that you aren't going to get repaid. If you just give them the money, they might spend it on something else and the bill won't get paid. After all, they are in trouble because they can't handle their money. When it's your money helping them out, take control of the situation and fix it. My suggestion is to take the bill out of their hands and pay it yourself.

If you help your kids with a loan, it makes you a creditor. Make sure you are willing to be a creditor and act like a creditor to your kids before you make that loan. Being a creditor means setting up a repayment plan that must be enforced. You will have to make collection calls and you will be viewed as the bad guy. They will play the "But I'm your baby" card and you will feel guilty. You will make them mad and they will make you mad. Your relationship will be damaged, maybe forever, over money.

A young woman on my TV show had borrowed money from both her father and her brother. Not a lot of money—only a few hundred dollars. She never paid them back. She was embarrassed. She became fearful of even making contact with them. She stopped all contact with them for years because she hadn't paid them a few hundred bucks. When I made her go meet with her father it was tough. He loved her and she loved him, but a wedge had been driven between them over a relatively small amount of money. How sad.

Be careful loaning your kids money. Know up front that it probably isn't going to end well. Be prepared for that outcome. Then ask yourself whether it's worth it. It might be better to just give them the money.

Before you help your kids, sit down with them and see if you can advise them on how to help themselves. Sometimes, that's when they learn the most.

Bounce some checks—become a cop.

My son Tyler is a police officer in Phoenix, Arizona. I am very proud of him. He is great at what he does. On top of all that, he loves being a cop. How did it happen? Money. Tyler, as a teenager, was a less than responsible human being. He played a bit too hard and didn't take anything very seriously. He had a job that he went to and worked pretty hard at. He was enrolled in a college that he didn't go to and didn't work very hard at. Instead he partied with his friends. And when he didn't have the cash to party, he wrote a check.

The problem was that the money wasn't always there to cover his checks. One time he wrote an 85-cent check for a highway toll. The check bounced twice and ended up costing him over $80, which he also didn't have. After a couple of months of this I found out he had about $800 in bad checks and was in serious trouble. He came into my office and laid it all in front of me and said, "Dad, I have messed up." (Only his language was a bit more explicit.) After reviewing his predicament, I said, "Yes, you have." (Only my language was *much* more explicit.) He said he had decided that he needed to get his life in order and wanted to join the U.S. Army. At that point, we weren't in any kind of war and I thought it was an excellent idea for him. I told him I would bail him out of his $800 of stupidity if he would enlist. He agreed and off we went that very day to the army recruiter.

Tyler flourished as a soldier. He went from the most undisciplined kid to the most disciplined man I have ever seen. After nearly eight years in the army, he wanted to get out and be a cop. Now he is. Why? You can say it was his destiny. Maybe. But I believe it was because of $800 in bounced checks. Yes, I helped him by paying the

$800. But he recognized his irresponsibility and knew he needed discipline in his life. He came up with the plan to fix his life. That decision, which was based on a money problem, shaped the rest of his life in a very positive way.

Cosigning.

Again, be careful. I've done it with both of my boys and it worked out. But I was lucky. My boys might mess up and screw over their credit card companies, but they would never even consider screwing over their dad. That is more a reflection of our relationship, though, than it is the money or the cosigning arrangement.

Your kids are not entitled to your money when you die.

My goal is to spend every dime I have left on the last day I'm alive. Why not? I earned it, didn't I?

"But, Larry, it's important to leave your children something."

You are absolutely right. But it is not important to leave your kids money. It is important to leave your kids with the confidence they can earn their own money. It's important for your children to know that you loved them enough to make sure that you provided for their education. It's important that you demonstrated your own ability to live to the fullest of your potential. It's important to teach your kids how to earn money, spend money, invest money, and enjoy money. It is not important to leave your kids any money.

SHOPAHOLICS AND ENABLERS. ✓

People shop for lots of reasons. They do it to feel better about themselves, to be somebody they really aren't, and out of a sense of entitlement. They do it to relieve stress, because they are happy, and because they are sad. Some people shop and spend simply out of habit.

The issue I see the most is that people shop to escape. They can't face their real lives, and shopping brings them some temporary comfort from their lousy relationships, their self-esteem problems, and even their lack of money. I worked with a guy who told me he went shopping because it made him feel better about the fact he had money problems. Money problems that existed because he shopped too much!

There are also people who are addicted to shopping. On *Big Spender* I meet lots of them—people who shop every single day. For anything. Life has no meaning unless they are spending money. Even a quarter. As long as the money leaves their hands and goes into the hands of someone else, then they think they are in good shape.

A shopping addiction is just like an addiction to cocaine. And it is cured in the same way. You have to go cold turkey. One time I had a cop on the show who was in drug enforcement but also loved to shop. He couldn't seem to stop even after I had worked him over. He told me he thought a more gradual approach would work better for him. I asked him what his response would be if a crack addict told him the same thing. "I'm just going to gradually cut back until I don't do it any longer." He said that he would tell him, "Bullshit." Okay then, "Bullshit." You don't wean yourself off shopping. You just stop.

I am not an expert on addictions. If you are truly a shopping addict, then you need professional help. Get some. Search the Internet or make some calls and find someone you can talk to about your addiction. Try:

www.debtorsanonymous.org

www.shopaholicsanonymous.org

However, don't be so quick to think you have an addiction just because you like to shop. Some people who just don't have the personal discipline and self-control will play the addict/shopaholic card as an excuse for their inexcusable behavior. Regardless of the degree of your shopping problem, here are some things I have found to be helpful:

Stay away from stores.

If you were an alcoholic it wouldn't be a good idea to spend time hanging around bars, would it? And if you were an overeater, you'd avoid the all-you-can-eat buffets, wouldn't you? So if you have a shopping problem, stay out of the malls and places where you will be tempted to spend money! Stores are not the only place to avoid. Stay away from the television shopping channels and from eBay and other Internet shopping Web sites. Duh!

I counseled a woman who was such a shopaholic that I didn't even want her going into the gas station to pay for her gas because she couldn't do it without buying a magazine, a Coke, or a candy bar. Stores of any type tempted her that much. In addition to getting some counseling, my suggestion was to remove as much temptation as possible.

Get new habits.

Many people spend out of habit. They buy takeout on Tuesday nights. They get a latte on their way to work. On Saturdays, they go to the mall. They check their e-mail and then hit eBay, even though they don't want anything or need anything. Don't fall into this trap.

You especially need new habits if your situation has changed. You are used to shopping with your friends and going out to lunch or having a drink after work. But you got laid off or divorced or had a financial emergency, so your situation has changed and you can't do it any longer. Explain to your friends and replace that habit with a new one.

Try the library. When I suggested the library to a woman, she responded with, "And what would I do there?" I laughed in her face. I suggested she might try finding a book to read. She said, "Yuk!" I asked, how about the park for a walk? She made an ugly face at me. She loved walking around the malls but couldn't find the energy to walk around the park. Overweight, not very smart, and unwilling to do a damn thing about it.

I can't tell you what to do. Find something that doesn't cost any money that can occupy your time. Just don't go shopping!

Shop with a list, a budget, and maybe even a chaperone! ✔

I've said it before and I'll say it again: Don't deviate from your list or your budget for *any* reason. If you can't be trusted to go to a store by yourself, go with someone who can keep you on track and remind you that you are at the store to buy essentials.

Carry cash. ✔

I've already covered this one, but it is especially important for the shopaholic. If you have $25 in your shopping budget to buy a gift, then put that $25 in an envelope with BOB's GIFT on it and only use that amount of money. It's easy to spend $40 when you have budgeted $25 if you use a credit or debit card. Envelopes with cash will keep you in check.

A word to the shopaholic enablers out there:

I could just as easily be the host of a television show called *Big Enabler*. Shoppers almost always seem to have an enabler: someone who either encourages them to spend money or won't say no to them when it comes to spending money. The enabler doesn't have the guts or the willpower to say no to the shopper.

I worked with one couple in their first year of marriage. He handled the bills and couldn't tell his wife no because he felt she might think less of him as a man. He wanted her to have anything she wanted, and he'd lie awake nights trying to figure out how to pay for things. She was oblivious to the fact that they were one paycheck away from bankruptcy. When he finally fessed up to her about how he felt, she assured him that she loved him regardless. Then she felt bad for spending so much.

You don't do your family or friends any favors by letting them ruin their lives when you can stop it. That's not love. Have your own little personal intervention and deal with the issue. The shopper might get mad, scream and yell, and tell you it isn't any of your business. But a friend should always come clean and tell another friend the real truth. And couples in a relationship should have complete, open communications about money.

If you are the enabler to a shopper, then you can't be the chaperone when the shopper goes shopping. If you are the enabler, you shouldn't call the shopper to go to lunch. You shouldn't ask them to go to the movies. You must limit your contact to activities that don't cost any money.

CHAPTER SEVEN

NOW IT'S TIME FOR YOUR NEW BUDGET!

In order to get ahead, you must have a written budget for spending money. In the past, you spent what you spent based on your whims and short-term desires, with little thought to whether you had the money or not. You spent and then figured out how to pay for it based on your juggling abilities. And you ended up broke. So obviously that wasn't a good plan.

You have been living backward. You spend and hope your expenses match your income. It is time to stop living backward. You are going to *begin* your budget with your income rather than finish your budget with your income.

Stop living backward and begin to live forward.
***Begin* with the end in mind.**

Here is your goal: Live on what you earn. Period. No excuses. No one cares about your excuses and problems. We are dealing with numbers here and the numbers don't have emotion. They are just numbers that have to balance. These numbers are what you live by.

In this book you have learned techniques for reducing your monthly expenses. You may have even taken the steps to do it. If you haven't, you should start immediately. You should have contacted your credit card companies and your insurance company. You should have disconnected your cable television and adjusted your cell phone plan already. You should have stopped eating out completely and cut back on groceries. You should have sold your toys and items you don't need in order to reduce your debt. Now you should be ready to create a budget.

We begin with the end in mind:

Monthly Income _____

This is ALL you have to work with. No more. This is it. It has to cover all of your expenses and leave you a bit to put in savings and a bit to give away.

MONTHLY

Mortgage or rent	_____	Other utilities	_____
Car loan #1	_____	Gasoline	_____
Car loan #2	_____	Groceries	_____
Personal loans	_____	($50 per person per week)	
Other loans	_____	Eating-out	_____
		Gifts	_____
CHARGE ACCOUNTS:		Dry cleaning	_____
MasterCard	_____	Health club	_____
Visa	_____	Hobbies	_____
Discover	_____	Vacation/travel	_____
American Expresss	_____	Clothes	_____
Other credit cards:		Entertainment	_____
#1	_____	Personal care	_____
#2	_____	Pet care	_____
#3	_____	Charity	_____
#4	_____	Medical	_____
#5	_____	Savings/ investments	_____
		(10 percent of your income is the goal)	
MONTHLY EXPENSES:		Church/charity	_____
Insurance	_____	(10 percent of your income is again the goal)	
Electricity	_____		
Gas	_____	Alimony/child support	_____
Water and trash	_____		
Telephone	_____	Any other debts or expenses:	_____
Cell phone	_____		
Cable television	_____	**TOTAL DEBTS AND EXPENSES**	_____
Internet	_____		

This total must not be more than your income. If it is, go back and adjust. Get ugly and make it fit.

"But how??!!"

I don't know and I don't care. You can't survive spending more than you make. Make it fit. Keep slashing your expenses until you figure it out. Or earn more money. But please don't be stupid and cut back on your savings in order to keep your cable television. When you have cut the numbers until they fit within your income, live on what you earn. That is what responsible adults do. Be one.

"But I don't get to live very well based on this budget."

I once told a woman that she might end up having to eat wish sandwiches every day. She said, "What's a wish sandwich?" I told her that's when you have two pieces of bread and you *wish* you had some meat to go between them. She didn't think I was funny.

You'll be fine. This budget won't kill you. Will you die from doing this? No? Then don't worry about it. It's not forever. It's what you have to do until you stop being broke. In fact, this will do you a world of good. You will sleep better knowing that for the first time in a long time, you are living on what you earn. When you earn more money, you can live a little better.

ADVICE FOR WHEN YOUR LIFE TURNS AROUND.

Hire a professional.

Once you have money, hire a professional to help you with it. Here is the key to finding a professional to help you with your money: Make sure they have a lot of money. Never pay someone to help you manage your money if they have less money than you do. Hire a really successful rich person to help you with your money. Ask them how much money they have and how they got it. If they won't tell you, move on until you find someone you can talk to who will come clean with you. You can't get a bargain when it comes to financial advice. Be willing to pay to get someone who is good at it. One of the ways you will know they are good at it is if they are rich!

Enjoy your money.

When you are making good money and your bills are under control, then enjoy yourself. Go to the best restaurants you can afford. Dress the way you want and wear the best watches and jewelry you can afford to wear. Take great vacations. Give huge amounts to charity. Get a massage or have a facial whenever you feel you want one. You didn't bust your butt to get rich only to live like you are barely getting by. That's dumb and an insult to your progress. Just don't abuse your wealth. Always make sure that you follow the guidelines of saving some of what you make and spending less than you make.

PART THREE

PROOF THAT IT CAN BE DONE!

*From Getting by
to Getting Ahead
to Getting Rich*

CHAPTER EIGHT

INTERVIEWS WITH LARRY'S RICH BUDDIES

Tired of what I have to say? Maybe you don't even believe me. Want a second opinion? That's fair. I called a few of my rich friends to ask them how they got that way and if they had any lessons they could share. You should do the same thing. Call a handful of your really rich friends and ask them how they got that way. Wait, you don't have any rich friends? If you were rich, you would!

I chose these five people for one reason: None started out rich. They all came from humble beginnings, and now they are all millionaires. They've all been broke and desperate and figured out how to turn it around. I respect where they came from and how they got where they are. While each story is different, see if you can spot the similarities.

JOE

Professional speaker, author, entrepreneur, restaurateur, real estate investor

Like me, Joe grew up poor yet is now one of the most successful business consultants and speakers in the country.

Joe grew up on a little dairy and tobacco farm in Tennessee. He tells me that he was poor but he didn't really know it at the time. He wore clothes that were handed down from his big brothers. His mother bought groceries according to what was on sale that day. And his family never once took any kind of vacation.

In the fifth grade he got interested in books and started reading James Bond books by Ian Fleming. He didn't care so much about the spy stuff. He was more interested in where the stories took place. He read about travel and living a high-class lifestyle in places like Nassau, New York City, Paris, and Monte Carlo.

During high school, Joe would skip classes and drive to Nashville, about thirty miles from his home, just so he could drive through the richest neighborhood in the city—Belle Meade. He was a sixteen-year-old kid with nothing, from a little bitty country town, cutting class just so he could go look at big, expensive houses.

But more than big houses and travel to exotic places, money represented freedom from worry to Joe. His parents had to worry about money every day of his life, and he didn't ever want to live like that.

Joe went to a small college and got a degree in political science. He had a wide variety of jobs, including working on staff at the House of Representatives, booking bands in nightclubs, and eventually he became a real estate agent. He discovered he hated selling houses. However, one day he went to a real estate sales seminar and heard Tom Hopkins, one of the biggest names in real estate training and professional speaking at the time. As he watched Tom, he thought about what Tom did for a living: traveling around the country doing seminars and having a good time. He decided *that* was what he wanted to do someday.

It took him two more years to make the move, but one day he quit his job and started knocking on doors, trying to sell himself as a speaker and trainer. When asked what he spoke about, he would just ask, "What do you want?" He knew if he could get a few hours to read a book or two on any subject, he could put together a seminar on it. A few took him up on it, but he was barely making a living. He was broke and hanging on by his fingernails. Like most new small business owners, he was so busy trying to live on the little money he did make, he didn't save anything for taxes. So at the end of the year he would find himself, as he puts it, "in the fetal position on the floor facing a tax bill that there was no way in hell I could pay." But somehow he stuck with it—and because he refused to give up, things finally started to come together for him.

Joe told me that one of the biggest factors in his success story was that he decided to be better than the competition. The credo he lived by was "Know more than your competition; be quicker than your competition; and do more for the customer than your competition." When a company wanted a proposal for a consulting/speaking job, his competitors would send their proposal through the mail or, at most, via FedEx. Joe would scrape together his last two nickels, buy a plane ticket, and deliver his proposal in person. Because he went the extra mile, he usually got the job. Joe worked harder, studied more, and was obsessed with always getting better and out-hustling the other guy.

At that point in Joe's career, a typical job would be to drive for twelve hours to speak to the employees of a school system in Mountain City, Tennessee. The speech would be in the high school gym to teachers, cafeteria workers, janitors, bus drivers—everybody. But he was making as much as $300 a day and felt "ten feet tall and bulletproof." Joe said: "I kept slogging through the muck of the lousy motels and fast food and endless nights away from home. Persistence. There's nothing like it! Except for education. I read everything. Still do. Business books, *The Wall Street Journal*, music magazines, fashion magazines, *Architectural Digest*, *The Economist*—you name it, I read it." There are days Joe reads nearly every word of five different newspapers in addition to a stack of magazines.

Lastly, Joe told me that while he never had a written-down business plan, he did always have goals. He knew exactly what he wanted his life to look like and stuck with it until it did.

Joe now is one of the highest-paid, most successful speakers in the country. He regularly travels to all those places he read about in the Ian Fleming novels when he was a kid, and he lives in a big, expensive house in Nashville just like the ones he used to drive by when he cut class.

JOHN

Insurance agent, financial planner

John grew up in Fort Worth, Texas. His daddy was a Sheetrocker during the week to support his Sunday preaching job for which he refused to be paid. According to John, "In my family it seemed that being financially downtrodden was mistaken for righteousness." He told me that while they really didn't know any rich people, it could only be assumed rich people were sinful. His family's biggest financial extravagance was to eat at a hamburger joint once a month. In fact, he never had a steak in a restaurant until he was in college. But it was this lack of money that made his family totally focused on money.

He worked with his father every day after school and six days a week during the summer from the first grade on. By the time he was fourteen, he was a journeyman Sheetrocker and as good as any adult on the crew. Because Sheetrockers are paid by the job and not by the hour, John learned the free-enterprise system: The more you produce, the more money you can earn for your family.

At about this time, during one of his family's many financial crises, John promised his mother that someday he would be rich so she wouldn't have to worry about money ever again. He said it wasn't a flippant comment at all; it was a promise that he was resolved to make happen. John says of all the promises he has ever made and fulfilled, this one to his mother has been the most rewarding.

John worked hanging Sheetrock to put himself through college. Along the way, he started hiring other students to work for him. He said that it amazed him that people would work so hard for a "by the hour" job, never expressing any interest in his profits or losses or how his expanding business worked. They just wanted their pay for the hours they worked. But John still wanted to understand business well enough to get rich.

Though John was a music major who had grown up poor and never had any money or any training in business math, it all seemed pretty simple to him. "If I got paid two hundred dollars for a day's worth of work and I owed my helpers one hundred dollars, then I was a businessman. On the other hand, if I got paid one hundred dollars for the day's work but owed my helpers two hundred dollars, then I was a fugitive, as I did not have the money to pay them and they would probably kill me with their Sheetrocking tools." Therefore John learned how to calculate his profits and losses on an hour-by-hour basis to make sure there was enough money to pay his helpers. He would set certain financial targets, and if he met them, would reward himself with a steak dinner at a nice restaurant. Soon John was eating a steak every night.

John says that the simple math of being wealthy makes great sense to him. "If you're broke, then the cost of a hamburger seems very high. If you have tons of dough, the cost of that same hamburger seems insignificant." John said that as he made more money, things seemed cheaper to him. While the cost of the hamburger and other goods remained the same, loads of money seemed to make everything a bargain. John made the decision that he wanted to create a world for himself in which the cost of things was insignificant—a world where he was so financially successful that everything he wanted to buy would seem like a bargain.

John decided to study all the ins and outs of the money and prosperity game. He wanted to learn all he could about how to attain wealth and invest it wisely. John is now a financial planner specializing in older Americans whose net worth is in excess of 100 million dollars. John is fascinated by the commonalities of affluence he has learned from working with very wealthy people. According to John, he says it comes down to these few things: Competency. Hard work. Perseverance. Serve others according to their needs, not your own. Spend less than you make.

BRAD

Brad coaches and leads one of the top financial planning offices for a major firm in Canada.

Brad grew up in a house full of people: two siblings, a single mother, an aunt suffering from MS, plus a grandmother and grandfather all living in one small house with one bathroom. Brad's bedroom was a closet off the living room. According to Brad, "Love was plentiful, money was always tight." They felt it most on Thursday night because that was grocery-shopping night. Going to the store was always full of tension and stress because there just wasn't enough money to get what they wanted. So it was day-old bread, powdered milk, and orange crystals instead of orange juice. Those grocery-store experiences made him hate the feeling of not having money.

The defining moment for Brad was when he decided to stage his own personal hunger strike before Christmas. He thought if he didn't eat, it would save his family money so they could have more for Christmas. After three days of not eating, he couldn't go on and decided that money was not going to dictate his life, but his life was going to dictate his money.

Brad decided to become rich. He worked construction and lived above a funeral home for $100 a month rent. He moved on to retail so he could make a few more bucks to live and he could buy books. He made success and wealth a study course by reading at least fifty books per year. Looking back, he says he has spent at least $100,000 at Brad's University of Wisdom by investing in books and attending seminars. Even after becoming a millionaire, Brad still attends lectures and seminars all over the world to expose his mind to the world's great thinkers and leaders. He began by surrounding himself with like-minded people who would challenge him and force him to become more by expecting more from him.

Brad has kept a daily journal for twenty-five years. Give him a date and he can flip through his journals to tell you where he was, who he was with, what was said, and what he thought about it at the time. When I was writing my book *It's Called Work for a Reason!* I called Brad to ask him to review notes from a speech he had heard me give more than ten years earlier and to remind me of anything particularly good I had said. It only took a few hours before I had a list of things he had learned during my session that day. He also told me how well they had worked since. What a source of information your journals can be!

Brad is also a voracious goal setter. Every New Year's

Day he sits by the pool at some beautiful resort and makes a list of everything he wants in life. These goals include money, health, spiritual development, business, personal development, family, travel, and anything else that comes to mind. They are extremely specific, and he reviews them constantly to monitor his progress. He makes his kids do the same thing.

If you had asked Brad at the age of seventeen what his life would look like today, you would find that today it looks almost exactly as he pictured it. He knew what he wanted in a wife and he got it. He knew what he wanted his children to be like and he got that, too. He would have told you that he would have lots of money, ample time to spend it, and would give lots of it away to those who need it. He does. He would have told you that he would have enough money so he would never, ever have to worry about it again. He promised himself that he would surround himself with astonishing people whom he would be able to call friends. I am one of them and for that we are both better people.

Brad says, "My dreams are so precise I could draw an artist's sketch of all of them."

Today Brad lives like a movie star with the anonymity of a regular guy. He loves life and family and friends. He still laughs in the face of the naysayers. He has never given up on anything, and says he never will.

PEGGY

Real estate agent and developer

Peggy was born into a poor family. She describes her father as a "mean alcoholic," but when he was sober she was able to draw great self-confidence from him. As a child, people would ask her, "What do you want to be when you grow up?" She would spill out actress, airline stewardess, mother, dancer, veterinarian, scientist, archeologist, and any other thing that interested her at the time. But her father told her she could be whatever she wanted and she believed him. Everyone else told her to pick just one thing, but her father never limited her in any way.

When she was twelve years old Peggy began to "blossom" and her family didn't have enough money to keep her in bras. Humiliated, she told herself, "This will *never* happen to me again." Mine was a pair of blue jeans . . . Peggy's motivation was a bra.

Peggy graduated from high school in May and got married in July at the age of eighteen. Her first son was born six days after her nineteenth birthday. Within five years she had two more sons. At the age of twenty-six she found herself getting divorced from a man who promised that, if she left him, he would never pay her any child support. He was true to his word for the next eight years.

Peggy had never worked outside the home and had no skills of any kind other than typing, which she had learned in high school. So she rented an old typewriter, practiced her typing skills, and landed a job as a legal secretary after talking politics with the senior partner who interviewed her. After a week, they caught on that her skills were limited and fired her with two weeks' pay. But Peggy remembered thinking, "That was easy. I'll do it again!" And she did. She got a job making $475 a month gross income. She had no child support to help and her rent was $350 a month. To make ends meet, she sold everything she owned. A man she was dating at the time taught her how to deal poker. She landed a job dealing poker at night and worked as a secretary during the day. She was working two full-time jobs while trying to raise three small boys. But as Peggy puts it, "Those were dark days and now I'm grateful for the gift of desperation. I made up my mind to survive and I did."

Peggy found working full-time both day and night to be a hard schedule and a hard life for a young, naïve mother of three. So she turned her attention to a career in real estate since it offered not only an unlimited potential for income but also a flexible time schedule. At least she could work any eighty hours a week she chose to work!

When Peggy started selling real estate, she had been able to save only two months' worth of living expenses. Because she made only straight commission, she had to sell something fast. She sold a house for $19,500, giving her a commission of $585, which she split with her broker. A year later she bought her own house . . . pretty good for a girl who, only two years before, had never owned her own car.

Peggy now does what she does, not to survive but to help make people's dreams come true. She has a "love affair" with selling real estate. Peggy has come a long way from that first commission of $585. Her average commission now is over $20,000. She owns fifteen houses and regularly buys, renovates, and sells houses in addition to her regular real estate endeavors. She and her team are rated the top team in her market and she has a net worth of more than 2.5 million dollars.

RANDY GAGE

Entrepreneur, author, multimillionaire, world traveler

You will notice Randy's full name is given. He wanted it that way. Some didn't. Some multimillionaires wanted to keep their business to themselves and shared their stories with you simply because they are my friends and I asked them to. Randy's story is one he readily shares with people in his seminars and books.

Randy was the middle child of a single mother who raised three kids while knocking on doors selling Avon. So Randy began with nothing but a determination to better himself. He had some bumps in the road along the way, but he persevered not only to become a successful multimillionaire but also to help millions of other people reach higher levels of success through his books, seminars, and coaching.

The most important factor for Randy was making the decision to be wealthy. Even as a child, he hated being poor and swore that he would become wealthy. He told all his friends that he would be a millionaire by the time he was thirty-five. Guess what year he made it? You got it: the year he turned thirty-five.

Randy was a teenage alcoholic and then moved on to hard drugs. He was expelled from high school and at age fifteen he went to jail for a series of burglaries and armed robberies. Yet even in those troubled times, he had a belief that he would grow up to be wealthy.

It would be nice to say that as soon as he turned from a life of crime to earning an honest living, his fortunes turned around. Nice but not true. Even though he dedicated himself to hard work, things didn't change right away.

Randy didn't really have a clearly defined dream. He knew what he was running away from, but he didn't have a clear vision of what he was running to. Like most of us, he fell prey to the common beliefs, such as money is bad, rich people are evil, and it is somehow noble or spiritual to be poor.

As a result, he strove for success on a conscious level, working hard, opening businesses, and hoping for success. Yet he kept subconsciously sabotaging his own success. He failed in a lot of business attempts, all while ruining his health, relationships, and other areas of his life. He reached the breaking point when his business was seized by the tax authorities and auctioned off for debts.

He was left with no car, no money, no credit cards, and $55,000 in debt. He sold his furniture to pay the rent and slept on the floor. His life sucked. But he stuck with it, because by this time he had started to develop a vision of what his dream life could look like. He began a study of the science of prosperity.

He read hundreds of books and filled dozens of notebooks with the ideas he learned. He went to seminars and workshops and started really evaluating how he spent his time. He looked at the people he was hanging out with and decided he needed to change some of them.

He wasn't afraid to work longer and harder than other people were. He adopted the motto "I will do today what others will not do, so in the future I can do what others cannot do." And he made it come true.

Today he lives in his dream home packed with more designer clothes and shoes than an Armani boutique. He's in better health in his late forties than he was at twenty, and he arranges his entire business schedule around the schedules of the four softball teams he plays on. He has his "fleet" of sports and luxury cars downstairs and wakes up to a view of sailboats on the bay. In the winter, he's in Florida, and in the summer you'll find him in

Paris or Costa Rica. Now he travels the world, coaching others to reach success.

GREAT STORIES, HUH?

I love these people and their stories. You might say I am lucky to be surrounded by people like this. I am. The best part is that I could have taken another twenty minutes after calling these five friends and had five more just like them with great stories ready to help me out. You might be the kind of person who sees wealthy people and assumes these people are just lucky or that they inherited their money. The reality is probably that they worked their asses off to get their money.

Know what? You are surrounded by people just like these. They might not be multimillionaires, but I guarantee you they have stories of overcoming adversity that would encourage you. You probably just never took the time to ask for their stories.

You could be a person just like any of my friends. Your story can't be any more tragic or complicated than any of these. Even if it is, you can overcome it if you look at what they did and emulate the lessons learned.

SUCCESS ALWAYS LEAVES CLUES.

After reading hundreds of biographies of great people I have noticed that successful people are all very similar. Their stories contain common threads. The people we all look up to are rarely extraordinary people. Instead, they are regular people doing extraordinary things.

As you read the five stories about my friends, did you notice any similarities? There are many:

Each started with almost nothing.
Each faced adversity.
Each had every excuse in the world to stay
    broke, yet refused to.
Each made a decision to be wealthy.
Each worked smarter, harder, faster, and longer
    than their peers did.
Each studied success.
Each had goals they were willing to take action
    on.
Each of them stuck with it even when it sucked.

Take a good hard look at your life. Then look at the similarities above. Now go to work. No excuses and no whining. Use these stories to inspire you to better things. It's not about talent or being special. It's about a willingness to do what it takes!

CAN YOU DO IT?

Of course you can. I've never met anyone who couldn't do better, and you are no different. You can do it. But that isn't really the question. The question is, *will* you do it? It's never about whether you *can* do it—it's always about whether you *will* do it. If you are sick of just getting by, will you change that and begin to get ahead? I hope you make that decision.

How far ahead is up to you. Following my plan *can* make you rich. But rich is up to you. Millionaire is up to you. You get to choose how far you take these principles. The principles never change, only the number of zeroes you put behind your net worth.

It won't be easy. It will sometimes be embarrassing. It may never be perfect. But it can be done. Now you know what it takes. The reality is that it's hard. It is hard to achieve prosperity at any level.

When you look at your life, your job, and your bank account, you might think that being rich or even getting ahead is impossible. If you *think* it is impossible, then it is. Stop thinking that way. If you *say* that it is impossible, it is. Stop talking that way. If you *act* as if it is impossible, it is. Stop acting that way.

To achieve the impossible requires discipline. We aren't a society that believes much in discipline. Discipline requires work—a daily commitment steeped in action in order to achieve your goals. That's my problem with goal setting. Too much focus on the goal and not nearly enough focus on the daily commitment or the action necessary to achieve the goal.

MY LESSON IN IMPOSSIBLE.

I grew up on a farm called Henry's Bantam Ranch. We had over a hundred varieties of bantam chickens. We also had rabbits, goats, pigs, cows, pigeons, horses, and other assorted animals and birds. One day a new calf was born and even though I was a little boy, I could pick it up and carry it around. My dad told me if I picked that calf up every day of its life and never missed a day, even when that calf was grown I would still be able to pick it up. I was skeptical. He explained to me that the calf would grow just a little every day but it wouldn't grow so much that I couldn't pick it up the next day. He said that if I ever missed a day for any reason, I wouldn't be able to do it. This seemed impossible to me. I looked at that calf's mother and she weighed about 500 pounds. I couldn't imagine picking up a 500-pound cow, but I always trusted my dad, so I told him I would do it. I picked the calf up and said to myself, "Day one." The next day, I went out to the barn and again picked up the calf. No problem. "Day two." The next day I did the same thing. I did it for about a week with no problem at all. Then it rained and I got busy and I had to play with my friends and I missed a day.

The next day I went to the barn and it was really hard to pick the calf up. My dad just smiled and said, "You can't miss a day. If you want to do the impossible, you can't miss a day." Then I got busy again and missed a couple of days. When I went to the barn the next time with my dad, I couldn't pick the calf up. No matter how hard I tried, I couldn't do it. My dad just laughed.

If I had continued every day with that calf, I have no idea if I would have been able to pick it up when it weighed 500 pounds. After all, a 500-pound cow is hard to get your arms around. But I still never forgot the lesson. If you want to achieve the impossible, you can't miss a day. It's the daily discipline, the daily work that makes achieving things possible. The impossible doesn't care whether you are busy, it doesn't care whether it's raining, or you don't feel good, or if you want to play with your friends, it still requires you to do all you can every day.

Maybe getting rich seems impossible to you. Maybe just getting back to even seems impossible for you. I remember when it did for me. The whole concept might be something you just can't get your arms around. It doesn't matter. You still have to work on it every day. You have to spend a little less, save a little more, pay a little more on your debt, read a little more, do a little more, and you have to do it all *every day*. You can't miss a day.

YOUR FINAL EXERCISE.

Now you know what it takes to go from getting by to getting ahead. You just have to make the commitment to do it. But a commitment only to getting ahead is just the first step to a life of financial security. I want you to be inspired to take these principles to the next level: getting rich. You deserve it. You deserve the peace of mind that comes from being rich.

Remember how I became rich? I made the decision. All of my rich buddies, Joe, John, Brad, Peggy, and Randy, made that decision too. Now you need to make that decision.

Take a minute and write down your decision to be rich. It's not enough to say it in your mind or to even say it out loud. Make it real by writing it down.

MY PERSONAL DECISION TO BE RICH:

_____
_____
_____
_____
_____
_____
_____
_____
_____
_____
_____
_____
_____
_____
_____
_____
_____
_____
_____
_____
_____
_____
_____
_____
_____
_____
_____
_____
_____
_____

Now sign it. This is your contract with yourself. This is a deal you are making with yourself and your future. You aren't making a deal with me. Your decision to be rich has nothing to do with me. It has to do with you. View this decision to be rich as a binding contract. You might be saying, "This is stupid. Who will know if I keep the contract or not?" Only you will know. You are the one who has to look yourself in the eye.

Since you probably just skipped this final exercise, stop and go back and write down your decision to get rich. Date it and sign it. And never forget:

A deal is a deal.

Larry's Twelve Ways to Go from Getting By to Getting Ahead

1. Know where you are.
2. Take responsibility for the situation.
3. Feel bad about it. Experience remorse.
4. Make the decision for things to be different.
5. Know exactly what you want your life to look like.
6. Create an action plan to get there.
7. Know what you are willing to give up to get what you want.
8. Spend less than you earn.
9. Figure out ways to earn more.
10. Stop all unnecessary spending.
11. Pay off debts as quickly as possible and only go into debt for things with long-term value.
12. Build a cushion. Save!

"Live long and prosper."

The Vulcan Salute, *Star Trek*

ACKNOWLEDGMENTS

To my rich buddies who contributed their personal stories to this book. Their friendship is a constant inspiration to me.

To my boys, Tyler and Patrick, who have always been proud of me and let me know it. I owe them big for that.

To my wife, Rose Mary, who loves me in spite of myself.

To my mom and dad, Dorothy and Henry Winget, who taught me to tell the truth, to be honest, work hard, and take responsibility: the real keys to success.

To Vic Osteen, my manager and friend, who knew me when I was a nobody and helped me become a somebody.

To A&E for picking me to be the host of *Big Spender*.

To NorthSouth Productions for producing *Big Spender*. They always make me look good and are simply the best to work with in every way.

To my friends at Gotham Books: Bill, Erin, Jessica, Lisa, and Beth. They are great folks who get me and what I do. They are a terrific team and I appreciate being a part of it.

FREE VIDEO DOWNLOAD:
Five Financial Lessons from Larry

To receive your free gift for purchasing this book, go to

www.YoureBroke.com.

You will find instructions for downloading your free video of Larry discussing key principles from the book and more. You'll actually get to see the tools discussed in the book and hear Larry talk about changing your financial future.

Plus, you will receive some extra bonus gifts just for visiting the site. You can even download the budget page from the book so that you can begin the process of getting ahead today!

Be sure to have the book on hand when you visit the Web site and are ready to download the video, as it contains the secret to downloading your free financial lessons.

w w w . Y o u r e B r o k e . c o m

Larry Winget is the author of the *New York Times* and *Wall Street Journal* bestseller *It's Called Work for a Reason! Your Success Is Your Own Damn Fault* (Gotham Books, 2007) and *Shut Up, Stop Whining, & Get a Life: A Kick-Butt Approach to a Better Life* (more than 100,000 copies sold). One of the country's highest paid professional speakers, he also stars in A&E's reality series *Big Spender* and is a featured guest on CNBC's *The Millionaire Inside*. He lives in Paradise Valley, Arizona, with his family.